# THE PROFESSIONAL PHOTOGRAPHER'S BUSINESS GUIDE

# THE PROFESSIONAL PHOTOGRAPHER'S BUSINESS GUIDE

by Frederic W. Rosen

AMPHOTO
AMERICAN PHOTOGRAPHIC BOOK PUBLISHING
*An imprint of Watson-Guptill/New York*

*For Mara Beth*



First published 1985 in New York by AMPHOTO,
an imprint of Watson-Guptill Publications,
a division of Billboard Publications, Inc.,
1515 Broadway, New York, NY 10036

**Library of Congress Cataloging in Publication Data**

Rosen, Frederic W.
Professional photographer's business guide.

Includes index.
1. Photography—Business methods. I. Title.
TR581.R67 1985 770'.68 85-1388
**ISBN** 0-8174-5550-7
**ISBN** 0-8174-5551-5 (pbk.)



Manufactured in the United States of America

1 2 3 4 5 6 7 8 9/90 89 88 87 86 85

"How did you become a professional photographer?" asked the student. He was speaking to Phillipe Halsman, a famous photographer known as much for the quality of his wit as the quality of his work. Halsman answered, "In the same way people get into most creative things. First, for my own pleasure, second for the pleasure of my friends and third, by *charging* for it."

# CONTENTS

# INTRODUCTION

"Just what the world needs! Another guide to professional photography," my friend Alex complained to me over the phone.

Alex is a photography magazine editor who has a cynical streak a mile long, but his point was well-taken. If you browse the shelves in your local bookstore, you'll find photography books written by photographers, photography writers, writers who are also photographers, photographers who are also writers, photographers who hire ghost writers, and sometimes writers . . . but you get the idea.

I've worked in the photography business for six years, beginning as a public relations account executive, representing a large camera manufacturer. Later, I was the editor of *Studio Photography*, a trade magazine for professional photographers. Now, I am a photography writer and photographer for a range of publications, including *The New York Times*, *Popular Photography*, *Lens'On Campus*, *The Rangefinder Photo District News*, and in the general press, *The Saturday Evening Post*, and the Sunday magazine section of the New York *Daily News*. In short, I've been around.

Sometimes, I feel like the Philip Marlowe of the photo industry, especially when I'm attending a press conference where a camera company is introducing a new camera body. But these press conferences are light years removed from the professional photographer who's first starting out in business. The camera companies are there to sell equipment. While they offer technical advice to pros, they won't tell you how to establish your own photography business.

For advice, you could try other photographers who've already turned professional. Many of them, however, won't want to share their trade secrets. They fear more competition in a market that's already heavily saturated with photographers. If you are lucky enough to get a professional photographer to talk, he may be so interested in talking about what a success he is that you learn nothing to help you out in your new business endeavor. Once again, you're out in the cold.

Many books offer false encouragement. They promise to turn you into a professional photographer in thirty days, money-back guarantee. I can't do that. No one can, regardless of what they promise. What I can do is this: give you a *pragmatic* guide to establishing and maintaining a photography business of your own. That's what this book is about.

# CHAPTER ONE

# MAKING THE RIGHT DECISIONS

---

*"You have to know how to do everything, from organizing your studio space to bookkeeping, in order to be a successful photographer."*

*—Don Banks*

## THE BUSINESS OF PHOTOGRAPHY

Photography is a rough business. I've "broken bread" with hundreds of photographers in the last six years, from New York to Alaska. Not one of them would disagree.

What makes things so tough? Most photographers will tell you that there just isn't enough business to go around. In some instances, photographers get work because of their reputations even though the jobs should have gone to the more competent, though less known, photographers.

To illustrate the latter point, I know of a case where an established photographer was given a large fee to take a photograph of a famous building as part of a corporate promotion. He took the shot, but it turned out so badly that the public relations executive accompanying him had to go back and take the shot himself. The shot subsequently ran as a giant mural in Chicago's O'Hare Airport—under the photographer's name.

There are thousands of photographers who could have done a better job than the photographer who was hired on the basis of his reputation. Still, it was his reputation that got him the job in the first place.

In addition to competition, other roadblocks when you first establish a photography business are:

Getting the money to go into business in the first place.

Getting the contacts for jobs.

Dealing with rejection from art directors and other potential clients.

Handling irate clients, while keeping the lines of communication, which lead to further jobs, open.

Getting cooperation from uninterested models.

Dealing with self-doubt, the bane of any creative individual.

Despite these obstacles, you should not be deterred from beginning a career as a professional photographer. Obstacles exist in any business, creative or otherwise, and photography is no exception. If you're technically competent and have a modicum of talent, you'll make it. At worst, you'll always be able to at least make a living as a professional photographer. At best, you'll get rich. If you're in-between, what's wrong with being, as my mother says, comfortable?

Still, technical competence, talent, determination, integrity and the most important ingredient—luck—aren't enough to become a successful photographer. Listen to what Don Banks has to say:

"Any artist without business ability may possibly find himself working as a clerk, or in some other non-creative job." (Banks asks that all clerks should write to me instead of him, since I'm doing the quoting.)

Banks ought to know. He's a very successful commercial photographer who specializes in what can only be described as elegant book-cover illustrations for both softcover and hardcover books. Yet, he wasn't always so successful.

Before becoming a professional photographer, Banks was a graphic designer in Philadelphia. In his spare time, he shot figure and fashion photography. When he, like many of you, realized he had a real talent and love for creating photographic images, he decided to make money doing it. He packed his bags and traveled ninety miles north to New York City to try his hand at being a pro, in the country's toughest photographic market.

Immediately, Don Banks came up against the proverbial stone wall. Without a reputation preceding him, he found the good jobs going to the already well-established photographers and their progeny, the assistants who worked with them. Many of these assistants had been trained at the country's top photography schools, like Rochester Institute of Technology, NY and Brooks Institute, CA.

Banks was able to break in after paying his dues—in short taking jobs he really didn't want—until he could do the work he is doing today. Still, without his business acumen backing up his photographic talent, Banks believes he would have failed.

How do you learn to "do everything," specifically how to break in, establish, and keep a professional photography business going? That's where this book comes in.

On the basis of my own experiences in photography, and that of others experienced in the field, we will provide you with a "road map" for your photographic odyssey. The idea, of course, is not to make it a long trip fraught with peril, but one that leads to success as fast as possible.

A warning—this doesn't mean that simply by reading this book and following everything in it, you'll automatically make it. There's one *intangible* quality anyone needs for success and that's luck. You can't be born with it, you can't buy it, you can't sell it, but "it" is there. It is pragmatic of me to say that the longer you work as a professional photographer, the better the possibility that you too will, at some point, be in the right place at the right time. That's my definition of luck. At that point, you'll land the big account (really), or suddenly discover something that makes your photographs reach a higher level of perfection, leading to increased sales.

## DEFINING YOUR PHOTOGRAPHIC GOALS

In order to be successful, the first thing you're going to have to figure out is what type of photography you want to do to make a living. After all, whether you're a professional photographer or not, you're still going to have bills to pay.

For the moment, forget about any idealistic goals regarding your photography. Forget about your dream to become the next Margaret Bourke-White, the next Arnold Newman, or the next Ansel Adams. Ask yourself the basic question: how am I going to support myself as a professional photographer?

Look around you. The first decision is whether to become a professional photographer in your home town or to go someplace else. So, if you live in a rural farming community in Iowa near a town of 9,000 people, there *may not* be enough to make a photography business grow and prosper. You're going to have to move where you can.

The same decision applies to city dwellers. I remember interviewing a prominent fashion photographer years ago. He said that he was advising budding photographers to try Houston instead of New York because there was too much competition in the Big Apple for novices to survive. I don't necessarily agree with him, but it could come down to an example as basic as this. Supposing you plan to open a wedding photography studio in your neighborhood. But, the neighborhood already has three or four other wedding photography studios that are already established. Those photographers have cornered the bulk of the business. To try and compete with them at this point would be economic suicide. What should you do?

Your best bet would be to move your business to a neighborhood where there's little, if any, competition. If you do move, you may also find the commute back to the old neighborhood, where you still maintain your residence, is too long. Then, you'll also have to move your residence closer to your business.

Sacrifice. No, I am not trying to sound corny. But in both examples, sacrifice was involved to establish a business. Decisions like these may occur at various times in your career. And the sacrifice of moving to another place is probably the easiest one you'll have to make because the sacrifices just don't stop there.

If you have gone to the effort of relocating and then establishing a photography business, you are telling yourself the business, at the moment, is the most important thing in your life. You are telling yourself that in your soul, you are a photographer. To compromise that vision would be condemning yourself to a life of second-guessing, of self-doubt like, ". . . if I'd only hung in there, I would have been successful. . . ."

Please don't misunderstand me. I'm not suggesting that personal relationships and photography don't mix. If you don't have the outside stimulation of personal relationships, your work *will* suffer. What I am suggesting is that sometimes you may have to choose between your trade and your personal life. For instance, you may find yourself having to shoot a job rather than going on a date. Do you keep accepting assignments that interfere with your personal relationships?

Decisions like this one become easier as you begin to define your photographic goals. What is it that you're hoping to get out of photography? Is it money, fame, emotional and intellectual fulfillment, or a new sense of self? Most photographers, in my experience, would say money and fame, and everything they bring with it. Few would cite emotional and intellectual fulfillment as the primary goal of the process and creation of photography. Yet how could these photographers create such eye-catching, and in some cases, gut-wrenching images simply for money and fame? In order to be good they must *feel* it, regardless of the lack of personal insight into their motivation.

So, if you accept the proposition that good photography is an expression of self, how do you create and at the same time make a living? Can photography be a combination of art and commerce? You bet it can!

There is not one successful professional photographer I know who is not, at the same time, a good businessman. That means they understand the market they are creating for, whether it be the wedding, commercial, or fashion markets. At the same time, the photographer has to consider how ambitious he is.

## A REALISTIC APPROACH

Some photographers are satisfied shooting weddings, a facet of the photography business that is often considered an uncreative area. But, the photographer who feels he can create evocative wedding photographs, and at the same time make money, is being just as creative as the fashion photographer who is considered to be at the apex of his profession.

Aspiring to be a fashion photographer, however, rather than a wedding photographer, can be an unrealistic goal. There is so much infighting in the fashion business, among the fashion magazines and clients that commission the assignments, to the modeling agency and the models themselves, that the fashion photographer has to have cast iron nerves to get one assignment, not to mention building a business.

In general, it is much more difficult as a photographer deals with an outside party or parties in the creation of his photography. It is harder to please a client and continue to get assignments. In a photography business where there isn't as much outside input, and correspondingly fewer people to please with the photographs, the easier it will be for the photographer to function. However, there's a difference between functioning and thriving.

It is not uncommon for a commercial photographer, who does everything from shooting still-lifes for ads to shooting an occasional fashion shot, to make in the upper four figures for an assignment. And, that's only for one time rights for his photographs. He can resell them as stock and make even more money.

The established, successful fashion photographer can make four figures for a shoot. Calculate that over a 52 week period. If the photographer does four fashion shoots a week, billing $3,000 per job, at the end of the year he would have grossed $624,000. It's the rare "Mom and Pop" wedding photographer who grosses more than $80,000 a year, and that's with a lot of hustling, in a major metropolitan area.

Still, if you want to play it safe, choose a branch of photography where you know you can break in and establish yourself. There's always time to switch to another branch of photography once you get established and have a base to build from.

Having provided these cautious words of advice, let me present the primary exception. Simply put, if you are positive you have the talent to succeed relatively quickly in a more competitive and higher paying photographic area, you have no choice but to go for it.

Earlier, I said that in order to be a success, luck was the most important quality to have. This is true, but actually what is *almost* as important is the belief that you're the best at what you do.

Whether you really are the best is irrelevant. It simply means that you really believe you are and can convince other people who can give you business that you are. Once you get to the point where you're hired to do a job, you have to be technically competent. But I've seen many photographers who are barely that, yet they have such a belief in themselves (and some would call this a delusion) that they have convinced their clients they *are* the best. They keep getting the assignments, regardless of the fact that there are many photographers who are starving and could do a better job.

As an example, I once interviewed a photographer for an article that was meant to be a profile of the photographer and an insight into the type of work he did. When I arrived on the set to see the photographer work with his subjects, I found that he didn't even know how to load a camera, a simple SLR. His assistant did everything for him, and all the photographer did was shoot.

The subsequent photographs were in no way exceptional. Still, the reputation of this photographer led me to believe that I would be dealing with an artist. Really, the only thing artistic about him was his belief that he was the best, and his mouth. He had convinced all his clients that he was the best. To this day, he is in constant demand.

Aside from making people believe you're the best, or being exceptionally talented and actually being the best, there's a whole middle-ground of photographers with some degree of talent. Some of them make up for a lack of brilliance with a gritty determination to succeed.

A photographer who is average can make up for his lack of talent with a constant effort to improve himself, through continuous shooting and analysis of his photographs. And, by then taking the time to establish contacts, he can build his business to the point where his clients look upon him as one of the best.

*Introspection.* Now it's time to look inward even further and begin to analyze what your strengths are. Are you a "Charlie Hustle"? Are you a big talker with absolute confidence in yourself? Or, are you an individual who is really talented?

Most of us fall into some in-between category. You may be talented, to some extent a good talker, and have a drive to succeed. Perhaps you're talented but don't have the drive to succeed. You're waiting to be discovered. You're definitely not going to make it. The point is to recognize your strengths and weaknesses. Build upon your strengths and try to eliminate your weaknesses. This isn't pablum; it's pragmatic advice.

Such self-analysis is difficult because it's hard to stand back and view yourself with the proper perspective. For this reason, consider getting a second opinion. Ask your photography instructor to comment upon your photographs. If you don't have an instructor, try a local photographer. Such an opinion, which you don't have to accept if you don't want to, might give you an idea of what your photographic abilities actually are. This may also help clarify your goals.

As far as the assets and deficits of your personality, this is an even more personal area.

It is important to understand your personality. For instance, are you an introvert or an extrovert? As a businessman, you're going to have to have constant interpersonal contacts with clients who have to respect you. It's also nice to be liked, but respect for your talents and who you are as a human being, is more important. And, if you don't like and respect yourself, no one else will.

Parents and friends who are loving and supportive might give you some perspective, but they're always going to be careful about what they say, for fear of hurting you. So, try to seek out a person or persons who'll give you an honest and fair appraisal of who you are as a person, regardless of the extent of their personal association.

Lastly, listen to your instincts. While a second opinion about your work and yourself is valuable, *you* are the one who knows best. This "gut" feeling might be based upon intensive introspection that takes the form of internal conversations. You may also wish to make a written or typed list of your personal and photographic strengths and weaknesses to make your task a little less difficult.

*Action.* With your self-analysis complete—that includes a clear idea of the kind of photographs you want to take—the next step is action. What are your alternatives in the photographic marketplace? Specifically, what are the various photographic areas you can realistically go into now that you have made an objective study of yourself and your abilities?

**PHOTOGRAPHIC STRENGTHS**

- Excellent with Composition
- Technically competent
- Prefer working with products rather than models

**PHOTOGRAPHIC WEAKNESSES**

- Not enough understanding of black & white
- Find it difficult to accept criticism from peers and teachers
- Not comfortable giving models direction

**PERSONALITY STRENGTHS**

- Determination to succeed
- Confidence in personal abilities as a photographer
- Love to work alone
- Like and respect myself

**PERSONALITY WEAKNESSES**

- Hate taking direction
- Sometimes become self-centered and self-absorbed

**CONCLUSIONS**

While I have all the skills to succeed as a professional photographer, as well as self-confidence, I find it difficult working with and taking direction from people while doing a shoot. I must find a photographic category where my strengths will be put to good use, while my weaknesses will not diminish my income or abilities.

**PRAGMATIC GOALS**

Try for catalog photography and, as interpersonal skills and contacts expand, think about becoming an advertising photographer.

*A written analysis of your photographic and personal strengths and weaknesses, supplemented by the conclusions you come to, leading to pragmatic career goals, might be set up like this.*

# CHAPTER TWO

# SURVEYING THE MARKETPLACE

The photographic categories I'm going to discuss are the ones *most* of you will aspire to. They are also the areas where the bulk of professional photographers work. These areas offer practical opportunities for photographers just turning professional.

## WEDDING PHOTOGRAPHY

To this point, I've probably mentioned wedding photography more than any other type of photography, and with good reason. The majority of photographers in this country working out of their own studio are wedding photographers. In fact, in the five boroughs of New York City alone, there are approximately 500 wedding studios. Why so many? Because people are always getting married and they *need* pictures, so the demand for pictures can be just as great or greater than the supply.

Another reason for the popularity of wedding photography is that you can make a good living doing it. However, you're not going to get rich. I do not know one wedding photographer who is rich. I know many commercial and fashion photographers who are. I also know a number of commercial photographers who started out doing weddings and then branched out into the more lucrative work they are doing at the present time.

Do not get the idea, however, that you can "slide" as a wedding photographer. You still have to deliver high-quality images that document an event in an effective and emotional way. If your photos are just technically competent but don't evoke any feelings, your business will lag and eventually go under. Word-of-mouth will do you in.

Word-of-mouth is perhaps more important in the wedding business than any other type of photography. Many of your jobs will be on the basis of recommendation. Start fouling up and the recommendations will dry up. The community where your business is located will come to realize that your work is not as good as other wedding photographers, who will subsequently get most of the new business.

How creative can you be when, day in and day out, you're shooting weddings? I've seen some wedding photographs that have actually evoked emotions in me even though I did not know the subjects. Other photographs I've seen have been hack work. Can't it get boring shooting essentially the same photographs on hundreds of jobs? The answer is yes, it can get boring, just like any job that involves repetition. What you have to do is to find a challenge in each wedding job, perhaps a different type of picture than the ones you've already shot.

I attended a wedding three years ago where one of the guests requested that the wedding photographer shoot a family portrait. The photographer agreed and went to the trouble of posing 42 people in three rows and then taking the shot. Try doing that during a wedding, with the band playing and people eating, and you can envision the difficulties. But, the photographer was not only pleased with the shot; he sold it as part of the wedding package to the bride and groom. Prints were subsequently made up and distributed to all 42 family members. As a postscript, the picture became especially important two years later, when one of those 42 died. It helped the grieving family to be able to look at that shot of a simpler moment when everybody was having a good time.

Wedding photography involves going on location. The wedding is divided by the photographer into three parts: the formals, where the wedding party poses for formal portraits, using indoor and outdoor settings; the ceremony, where the wedding vows are exchanged with complete documentation by the photographer; and the reception, where photographs are taken of bride, groom, and guests enjoying themselves during dinner and dance.

Usually, the wedding photographer charges a fee for his services. An additional fee is charged according to the size and amount of pictures, as well as the type of album (leather or otherwise) in which the photographs are mounted.

As I've mentioned, wedding photography can be creative. It is easier to get into than any other photography profession, and it can be used as a stepping stone to more lucrative and emotionally satisfying photographs.

Frequently, wedding "shooters" expand their services to cover other types of photography, including advertising, photographing art, catalogue, and fashion work, because they have the studio space, and the lighting and camera equipment to do more than one type of photography. Such expansion of his business is another way for the wedding photographer to make additional revenues. Still, the bulk of his income will come from his wedding shoots.

Since the wedding photographer usually works out of a storefront studio, he may also shoot formal portraits of children, families, and graduating high school and college seniors. The latter may also be shot at the local high school or college. Occasionally, the wedding photographer may also shoot team pictures at the local high school as well.

## SCHOOL PHOTOGRAPHY

School photography is often done by the wedding and portrait photographer, especially in smaller communities. But in larger communities, diversification is greater, so school photography is frequently done by a photographer specializing in this area.

What is school photography? Do you remember your days in elementary school, and a photographer would come to take class and individual portraits? That's one aspect of school photography.

The second aspect of school photography is senior portraits. These are photographs of graduating high school and college seniors that are taken either at the school or in the photographer's studio. The photographs are subsequently sold to the student for their own personal purposes. Usually, one portrait for each student winds up in the high school or college yearbook.

The third type of school photography is taking photographs of the athletic teams. A school photographer will go down to his local high school or college to shoot individual and group pictures of baseball, football, and basketball teams. Once again, photos are sold individually, and some of them also wind up in the school yearbook.

In order to shoot in a school, the photographer has to get permission beforehand. Usually, he'll have to agree to give the school a certain percentage of his profits for the privilege of shooting in the school, or trade his services at a later date for the permission to shoot.

The school photographer gets his business by going out and actively soliciting. He can simply make an appointment with a school's principal or whomever handles its business affairs, go in and try to arrange a contract to shoot the school's students.

Many school photographers do not restrict their team shooting to teams from local high schools and colleges. They will also shoot little league teams as well.

Again, permission has to be obtained in advance from the little league's board of directors to do the shooting. The business arrangement will be a similar one to the one negotiated with schools. A percentage of profits may be the fee for the privilege of shooting the league's kids. You may agree to provide your services at a later date in return for permission to shoot.

After the arrangements have been made and contracts signed (if necessary), the photographer notifies the coach of the shoot. The coach tells his players. The photographer than provides the coach with all the paperwork and the flyers explaining the service, which the players bring home to their parents.

When the player comes to the game the day of the "shoot," he has his order form filled out. He gives the check and the form to the coach, who then gives it to the team photographer. A few weeks later, the final photographs are delivered to the coach and he distributes them to his team.

One school photographer I spoke with had made a deal to shoot the local Triple A Minor League team of a major league franchise. He knew that the professional baseball players had the same needs as the amateur ones: they wanted to see themselves in uniform. So, he shot the ballplayers, and in addition to selling the pictures to them, the team subsequently sold the pictures to fans at the ballpark. Without a doubt, everyone profited.

## CATALOG PHOTOGRAPHY

Catalogs present a manufacturer's inventory or product line, whether it be furniture, clothes, glassware, gifts, handbags, home furnishings, chandeliers, ceramics, toys or watches. These products are photographed by the catalog photographer, and are then inserted into the catalog.

In addition to technical competency on a format other than 35mm, the photographer has to be versatile. He must become familiar with the product he's shooting, and how he can show it to best advantage on film. Ultimately, the catalog photographer must be able to sell the product through his photographs.

One of the drawbacks of catalog photography is the lack of direct public feedback. Feedback is actually received by the client, in the form of sales, and the word filters back to the photographer about how successful his photographs were.

The size of the job can range from something small, like a three-page brochure, to a thirty-two page catalog. Correspondingly, the size of the job will be determined by how big a line is to be introduced, and who the manufacturer is.

Major catalog houses have in-house photographic facilities where the beginning photographer can find work. As your business expands and you go out on your own, work will be generated by referrals and door-to-door salesmanship. How is this done?

The catalog photographer will show his work, which has been mounted in an attractive portfolio, to a prospective client. He will explain what he's done and what he can do. A portfolio that's continually updated will frequently result in new business.

Catalog photography is nearly always done in a studio, with a rare location shoot to utilize an unusual setting. Consequently, if you are going to break into this category, you're going to have to pay for things like studio upkeep, rent, insurance, and of course film, processing, and equipment.

As far as breaking into this field is concerned, major catalog houses, as I've already mentioned, are your best bet. They do a diverse amount of work, from tabletop set-ups to fashion work, so you get a lot of experience that will stand you in good stead when you decide to go out on your own.

## BOOKCOVER ILLUSTRATIONS

Photographs can also be used as a model on which bookcover paintings are based. The photographs shot for bookcover paintings never actually appear as they were shot, on the bookcover. They are enhanced by the artist. The photograph is taken to fit the specifications of the art director for the publishing company. This is then handed over, unretouched to the artist. Both the artist and the photographer have been commissioned by the publishing house. The artist does a painting of what he thinks the bookcover should look like, using the photograph as a guide for the way a character looks, and for dress, props, and lighting. The painting is then reduced in size, type is added, and it then becomes the bookcover. The type of books utilizing this hybrid of photography and art are romances, action/adventures, and westerns.

You may be wondering why the publishing house doesn't just go with the straight photograph, however. The answer is that publishing houses consider these types of novels to be larger than life, and they want the bookcovers to reflect this. They don't consider photographs to be dramatic enough, but paintings are. Still, it's cheaper to have a photographer take a picture, which is essentially used as a model, rather than hiring models to be in the artist's studio every day that he's doing his painting.

Bob Osonitsch is probably the leading photographer in New York (maybe in the rest of the country) who does this type of work. Osonitsch has a studio divided into various areas. One area in his studio space includes full wardrobe and prop departments so he can dress and prop his models to look like the characters in the novels they are "portraying".

Osonitsch will rarely use an elaborate set during a shoot. For instance, if a loving couple is posed before a waterfall, the models will be called upon to act like they're at the location while the artist will paint in the actual location afterwards.

Osonitsch shoots in black-and-white and has his own processing machines on premises. This allows him to present the artist with a finished photograph in record time, something they appreciate when they have a pressing deadline to meet.

The photographer working in this area must have the ability to provoke mood and emotion with only his camera, the wardrobe, and props for support. He's directing the models like a movie director, so he has to be able to effectively communicate the emotional effect he's striving for.

Few photographers do this type of bookcover work. Frankly, Osonitsch and a few others have the market cornered. But I've never met an art director for a book publishing company who wasn't interested in looking at a new pro's portfolio when the photographer has some dynamite images to show him. Remember, getting your foot in the door is the first step in getting the job.

## BOOKCOVER PHOTOGRAPHY

For other genres of softcover books, actual photographs are generally used on the bookcover. Once again, it is the publishing house, through the art director, who commissions the photographer.

The photographer is then called in to confer with the art director. They jointly decide the direction the bookcover will take. It's up to the photographer to execute the idea. The photographer will also read or at least skim the book he's shooting, to get an idea of what it's about. This will give him ideas to tie in the photograph with what is happening in the book.

Once the photographer has his assignment and an idea of what he wants the bookcover to look like, he has to first construct the set he's going to need. If it's anything too elaborate, he'll go to an outside set maker. Occasionally, he may construct the set himself.

When a set maker is needed, the fee is paid from the budget the art director gives to the photographer for the entire shoot. This budget is based upon the photographer's estimate for the job.

When the set is made and delivered to the photographer's studio, the next thing the photographer has to worry about is whether or not he needs any unusual props. For instance, when Don Banks (the bookcover photographer I mentioned in the first chapter) was shooting a World War II mystery, he discovered that the key to the story was a pocketwatch with unusual design. He had to get a pocketwatch that matched the writer's description in the book, and then make up a special watch face that also matched the writer's description in the text.

On other shoots, Banks relies on a model maker to construct unusual props that cannot be obtained anywhere else. Once again, the model maker's fee is paid for out of the budget Banks works out and then receives for the entire shoot.

With props now set, Banks is free to call up his casting director who, in turn, calls the modeling agency and arranges for a model or models for the shoot, should they be needed. Sometimes, a simple photographic solution to the book's mystery, like the pocketwatch, is enough, and (except for the set) nothing else is required.

As you can see, shooting straight photographs for bookcovers is very creative and only one part of the job is taking the photograph. It's also a job where the photographer can easily see the results of his work at any bookstore that carries the books he's shot.

Because bookcover photography is a lucrative area for a photographer, it's also competitive. There are many more photographers aspiring to jobs than available jobs. But an art director I spoke with at Ballantine Books told me that he regularly looks at photographers' portfolios because he's always looking to hire photographers ". . . who can create good, clean images."

## AERIAL PHOTOGRAPHY

Have you ever wanted the thrill of hanging out of a plane while taking pictures? If that's something that appeals to you, consider aerial photography.

Aerial photography involves shooting images of buildings, factories, schools, freeways, and shopping malls for a variety of clients—real estate developers, your local chamber of commerce, corporations, and city governments.

Many of the photography studios that specialize in aerial photography are owned and operated by photographers who are also pilots. But, any photographer who gets an aerial assignment can fulfill the terms of his contract by renting a plane and a pilot's services, providing the client pays for both.

While there is a thrill element involved in aerial photography, from a practical point of view, I doubt the wisdom of embarking on a career in this area, especially when you're beginning your business. You have to develop confidence in your abilities, which is rather difficult when you're hanging out of the door of a helicopter at 2,000 feet. Everything shakes, including your nerves. You'll have more of an opportunity to develop your photographic skills with a variety of studio, or more sedate, outdoor assignments. Look at aerial photography as a possible adjunct to your other work, essentially a way of making extra money. If you rely on it for your sole income, however, you may starve.

## ARCHITECTURAL PHOTOGRAPHY

Architectural photography can be one of the profession's most creative outlets. To make a building appear attractive for instance, by shooting from different angles to give it an abstract appearance; to expose with different emulsions during various seasons and times of day to get dramatic lighting effects; to shoot an interior with a starburst filter, so the chandeliers in a hotel's ballroom sparkle, these are just some of the things that an architectural photographer does.

Clients can range from hotel and motel owners who want attractive pictures of their properties to include in their advertising brochures, to architectural magazine publishers who are always looking for interesting photographs. In between, you'll find that landscape gardening firms, interior design firms, custom-home builders, restaurant owners, travel and entertainment publications, and real estate investment syndicates all have need of architectural photographs.

In this field, the photographer is well paid, but the technical requirements are great. Not only do you have to be familiar with 35mm SLRs, you also have to know how to use large format cameras, which most jobs require.

Sometimes, the photographer may trade his photographs and expertise for goods and services. For instance, I was once hired by the Cunard Line to photograph the interior of their flagship, the Queen Elizabeth II.

The deal was simple. I take the photographs in return for a free cruise. I agreed, but made one important provision—every shot had to be listed on paper *before* I got on the ship. I did this because if I hadn't, I could have been asked by one of the Cunard executives to take more shots that I'd contracted for once I was on the ship.

Everything worked out. I took the shots, I had time to enjoy my cruise, and Cunard liked the photographs.

Like annual report work, architectural photography is not a category that beginning photographers flock to. It's an essentially lonely job because once you get the assignment from the client, you go out and shoot on your own. There's no one to do the make-up or wardrobe on the exterior of a building, though you may have an assistant set up an interior to make it look attractive. Unlike commercial or fashion photography where you may use models, there's definitely nothing glamorous about architectural photography.

However, architectural photography can be artistic. If the photographer has an intuitive or studied understanding of architecture, he can make his photographs into works of art. He can make the simplest building look like the Taj Mahal on a sunny day. It's just a question of understanding shape and light, and applying the photographic skill to enhance it to make a great photograph.

## ANNUAL REPORT CORPORATE PHOTOGRAPHY

More than any other kind of photography, shooting the annual report of a large corporation is overlooked by new pros. Why? Because, unless you're a shareholder in a corporation, you rarely see an annual report. Shooting the photographs in the annual report, which can be heavily industrial in nature, is not something you're going to be thinking about when you make your decision to go into business.

One question you may have is, who pays attention to the photographs in annual reports? There are two answers. First, the executives of a large corporation want quality images to accompany their annual report to the stockholders and shareholders. These executives are important, powerful men who are sometimes in a position to recommend you for more jobs.

The company's art director or designer is also important. He frequently hires the annual report photographer, and is often the one to offer suggestions and criticisms relating to the project.

Magazine and newspaper photography editors are the second group interested in these photographs. They are always looking for original, technically competent photographers, and a portfolio of annual report photographs that are dynamic could lead to editorial jobs.

To give you a better idea about annual report work, let me talk about Burt Glinn. Glinn is a famous photojournalist who became an annual report photographer in the 1960's.

He is frank about the change in his work. He says that one of the primary reasons he got into annual reports was because he'd grown used to a certain style of living and didn't want to abandon it. He knew it paid well, and through connections he'd developed as a photojournalist, he began getting jobs shooting annual reports.

Glinn feels annual reports are collaborative efforts. You need a client who understands an annual report and what it's supposed to say about his company and employees. You also need a good designer, someone who, if he has to, can take mediocre pictures and by creating an eye-catching layout, by cropping the pictures, and by using interesting background colors on the page, make those pictures look great.

A good example of this collaboration is Glinn shooting for Warner Communications. An assistant to the corporation president works with Glinn to decide the overall direction the photographs will take. Another executive sits down with Glinn and explains the specific aspects of the corporation that have to be photographed. In this way, Glinn, gets into the decision-making process.

Glinn is also frank about problems that can develop during an annual report shooting. In this case, his ability to improvise (an important attribute of the annual report photographer who shoots on location where he cannot control things like he could in a studio) helped him out of a jam.

Glinn was assigned the job of shooting a report for a company that manufactured a valve used in open heart surgery. So Glinn and his assistant went to Japan to shoot during an actual operation.

When they got to the client's headquarters in Japan, they found out that we were supposed to stage a *mock* operation. Glinn was taken to a nearby hospital to a rented hospital room. When he got to the room, it was empty! No instruments, no patient, no nothing. Glinn commandeered some gowns, masks, gloves, and instruments. He got some of the client's employees to dress up as doctors and nurses, while another employee lay down on the operating table, and was draped like it was an actual operation. Finally, Glinn had the fellow playing doctor bend over him with the heart valve in his hand, like he was going to place it in his chest. The final photograph looked very convincing.

## PHOTOJOURNALISM

Slick, awkward images of celebrities caught off guard, and photographs of people involved in their own grief who would rather be left alone are not considered true photojournalism.

Photojournalism, at its best, is a penetrating glimpse into a social problem by isolating one facet of it. For instance, photographer Mary Ellen Mark did a photo series about the street life of Seattle, Washington. In one photo, a pathetic-looking boy, part of a street gang, surreptitiously shows a gun which he takes out of his coat, to the camera. Behind him, a friend stands watching (see page 48).

The effect is shocking. Here we are watching the origin of a potentially a criminal act. Such devastating statements with the camera are the hallmark of good photojournalists. They help us to think about the things around us.

While photojournalism, especially on a newspaper, is not an exceptionally well-paying position, it is a highly competitive one. The good photojournalist has to compete against the type of photographer, like the paparazzi I mentioned at the beginning of this section. But, everyone wants to shoot celebrities. Few photographers want to or are good enough to record feelings with their camera—to make a compact, nonverbal statement. It may actually be easier to break into doing socially-oriented photojournalism for these reasons.

Magazines and newspapers are the principal outlets for these photos. Some photojournalists, the really good ones, get representation by a photo agency like Gamma/Liason. The agency sends the photographer out on a specific assignment. The agency then markets the photos to their editorial clients, saving the photographer the job of being a marketing expert. For this service, the photo agency receives a certain percentage of the sale that the photographer and photo agency agree upon in advance.

If you choose to market your photographs yourself, *Photographer's Market* and the *Writer's Market* are good reference books to consult. The books, published by Writer's Digest Books, contain listings of magazines and newspapers that will buy photographs. (see Appendix)

## PUBLIC RELATIONS PHOTOGRAPHY

Public relations photography involves shooting a variety of professional functions, including opening-night parties of Broadway shows, to corporate Christmas parties.

I met Kathy Blavis at a party honoring the hundredth anniversary of a firm called Engineering Information. She not only shot public relations at parties, but she also did portrait work as well. She rounded out her photographic activities by shooting photos of theatrical and dance companies that are used for promotional purposes.

That's precisely the purpose of public relations photography: to promote a product, whether it be a dance company, or a firm like Engineering Information. The photos can be used in newspapers, on billboards, outside theaters, or simply sent out as part of a general press release.

## EDITORIAL ILLUSTRATION

Editorial illustration encompasses photographs that help to illustrate an already existing article. For instance, the photographs I use to illustrate the "Camera" columns I write for The *New York Times* are selected, and sometimes shot, only *after* the column has been written. For a magazine article, the same process usually applies.

For instance, I recently had occasion to write an article about actors who were involved in businesses outside of show business. Pictures of the actors were required to accompany the text which I had already written. One of the actors I spoke to for this article was Patrick O'Neal who owns a number of restaurants in New York City. The magazine I'd written the article for, *The Saturday Evening Post*, asked me to go to one of O'Neal restaurants and take the necessary photograph, which, of course, I did.

More frequently, a magazine will assign a full-time photographer to take the shots. This type of work is obtained by making an appointment to show the magazine's art director your work, or doing it by mail via *Writer's Market* (see Appendix). Photography magazines, however, usually ask that the writer illustrate his own article.

## FASHION PHOTOGRAPHY

At the other end of the spectrum is fashion photography. The fashion photographer has to work with scores of people.

For instance, on any one shoot, where the photographer is shooting a fashion layout for a magazine, he will have to work with the art director at the magazine, who gave him the assignment and whose conception he is trying to realize. He will work with the make-up and hair stylists who get the models ready according to the photographer's instructions. The assistant helps the photographer with all the technical aspects of the shot, e.g. loading the camera, taking light readings, adjusting lighting, and so forth. Last, but not least, he deals with the modeling agency that books the models for the shoot, and the models themselves who must be posed by the photographer to convey the feelings he is looking for in the finished photograph. There may also be additional wardrobe people on the set to make sure the clothing—the principal subject of the fashion shoot—fits properly and always *looks* fresh, colorful, and comfortable.

As you can see, the fashion photographer must be an excellent communicator. He has to be able to take instructions as well as give them. He also has to be able to cope with the demands and inadequacies of his clients, and the emotional needs of the models, whose visions of themselves are reinforced by the photographs taken of them.

During the actual shoot, the fashion photographer has to be prepared to move things along quickly because models work on an hourly rate. Suppose a model is booked for three hours at $300 an hour. Because the model is lackadaisical, the shoot takes four hours. That's an additional $300 out of the client's pocket and possibly, the photographer's. The photographer has to be prepared to crack the whip.

Despite these drawbacks, fashion photography can be one of the most rewarding professions. It's creative; you get the opportunity to work with elaborate sets. Your work is admired by millions, and you can make millions, too. But you will need some influential business contacts to help you land the fashion "shoots" because the competition for them is so intense.

One final note about fashion photography and then I'll move on. This type of work requires an extensive amount of technical knowledge. Lighting the models to make them attractive is not easy. Many models look nothing like they appear in the finished photograph. It's the job of the photographer and the make-up artist to have models made up so they look attractive, and to shoot them in the most flattering way, which involves manipulating the lighting.

Posing will also be a prime factor in any successful modeling shoot because the model must be made to look natural—unless the opposite effect is desired. So, the photographer has to make the decision whether to shoot close-up or ¾ poses, full-figure, or an extreme close-up on just one of the model's features.

Bearing in mind that his photograph will, in all probability, contain copy (advertising or editorial in nature), the fashion photographer has to frame for this. Compositional elements including line, form, and color, only serve to make the photograph more exciting and sell the product.

## COMMERCIAL PHOTOGRAPHY

Next to wedding photography, the next largest group of working photographers falls into this category primarily because this encompasses any area in which the aim is to promote or sell a product.

The commercial photographer shoots a product for an advertisement that can appear in a variety of places: newspapers, magazines, billboards, brochures, and just about any printed matter where products are advertised, with the exception of catalogs.

The products can be eyeglasses, perfume, lingerie, furniture, food, in actuality anything someone is trying to sell. Some of these products lend themselves to photographs involving models, like lingerie and perfume, while others, like food, are generally shot as still lifes where the food is made to look incredibly edible.

The assignment for the commercial photographer can come from one of two sources: the art director at the advertising agency, or the client (or his representative) who contacts the photographer directly. In both cases, the photographer will be told what he is to shoot, what the photograph should look like, and what his budget is for the shoot.

Because commercial photography involves doing different kinds of shots, from still lifes to fashion, it's a great way to make a living and get experience at the same time. You can also make a lot of money when you work for bigger clients, like large corporations or advertising agencies. But, there's a major drawback to commercial photography—hustling for jobs.

Hustling is a way of life for the commercial photographer. He has the upkeep on his studio space to consider, and whether or not he's shooting, that upkeep has to be paid. This produces an incredible amount of pressure on the commercial photographer to be constantly working and seeking new jobs at the same time. Frequently, there's little time to put photographic artistry into the shot. Survival, *getting the next job*, obscures and mutes any attempt at art. To illustrate this point, I'm using two extremes.

I know one commercial photographer who lives in the photo district of New York named Hal Jordan (a pseudonym). He's more of a hustler than a photographer, though when he shoots, he shows real talent. Still, he's always barging in to art directors and others that he knows at ad agencies, and public relations agencies too, trying to get another assignment.

When Hal does work, he's usually got such a heavy deadline, there's not time to even eat. It's simply shoot, bring the next product in, shoot again, get the film down to the all-night processor, and then bring the finished photograph into the client in the morning. By that time, Hal is so tired, he can't go out to get new business. What happens when next month's bills come due? He may not have the cash.

Hal's personal life is strained, because he rarely has time for relationships. He's too busy hustling, which also causes him to wittingly and unwittingly, use his friends to get jobs.

Not a very pretty picture, is it? The fact that Hal is competing for jobs in the country's densest photographic market, New York, doesn't make matters any easier for him. Yet, if you asked him now why he got into photography in the first place, he couldn't tell you. He forgot someplace between last night's shoot and hustling for his next job.

Hal's other problem is that he's insecure, both in his perception of himself as a person and as a photographer. That's why he's always hustling and why many people don't like him. He doesn't like or respect himself.

Not all commercial photographers hustle as much as Hal, however. A few years ago, I interviewed a photographer named Bob Kiss. Kiss was an R.I.T. graduate who settled in New York City and became a commercial photographer.

Kiss is a go-getter, the type of person who believes in his talent and has the portfolio to prove it. While he still solicits new work, actually his "rep" does that (see Chapter 9), he has enough time to consider what he does a combination of art and commerce. If you look at Bob Kiss's photos, you can see that while he's selling a product, he's doing it artistically.

Kiss was also smart enough to realize the value of editorial exposure. He showed his portfolio to Andy Warhol's *Interview* magazine and subsequently shot many assignments for them. He later capitalized on the promotional possibilities, when an exhibit of his stunning *Interview* photographs ran in a New York photo gallery.

What's the difference between Bob Kiss and Hal Jordan? Why is one successful while the other struggles? If I had the definitive answer to that question, I could probably go into business and make a mint. But there are some basic conclusions we can come to.

Hal has allowed the business side of what he does to dominate his photography. He's forgotten that a photographer seeks to make a statement with his photographs, in addition to making money. In contrast, Kiss realizes he's in the business to help sell products, but he's going to do it in such a way that it artistically satsifies him, and hopefully, his client and the public. So far, he's been right.

Where did Hal go wrong? Can't he begin to put in the extra time on his jobs to make his photographs more artistic? He can, but he's so jaded at this point that the thought doesn't even occur to him. He's too far along to change. But the beginning photographer is not.

## STOCK PHOTOGRAPHY

Stock photography is an area where a photographer can either specialize, or make additional income by selling his work from other jobs.

Barry Winiker is a freelance photographer specializing in cruiseship and resort photography, which the stock houses refer to as destination photography.

Barry started shooting professionally ten years ago. In 1980, he began selling stock on his own, by getting leads from the travel editors he regularly did business with. Then, about two years ago, he began investigating in earnest selling to stock agencies. He used the book *Photographer's Market* (see Appendix) and other reference sources and made a list of 20 agencies that sounded like they might be interested in buying his work.

Before contacting the twenty agencies, he asked the travel editors he regularly did business with for their opinion, whittled the list down to four agencies, and sent out his queries. He found three agencies interested in his work, and he eventually signed with two of them.

Winiker emphasizes that you need at least 500 to 1000 transparencies to begin a relationship with a stock agency and then at least 1500 to 3000 on file. You keep adding month-by-month to see appreciable sales.

"I've found," says Winiker, "that most contracts with stock houses are from 3 to 5 years and on the average, the photographer gets 35% to 50% of the sale the stock houses make to a newspaper or magazine."

Winiker advises any photographers who want to sell stock to specialize in a specific area, like destination photography. Then, once you are established, which can take some time, you can branch out into doing other types of photography.

Miguel Martin is also one of the premier stock photographers in the country. Martin's "rise to fame" as a stock photographer is an interesting story. Originally, Martin had been a staff photographer at Macy's, the large New York City department store. He did a lot of portrait work, but this obviously required him to stay in one place. Martin loved to travel so he wasn't really happy with the arrangement. How could he combine his love of travel with his job—photography—and still make a living?

Martin decided to contact Image Bank, a stock photography agency. Martin found that there was an opportunity to do the two things in life that he loved most: travel to the far corners of the world and photograph.

Like most stock agencies, the Image Bank sells photographs to anyone from advertising agencies to magazines. But what Martin diligently noticed was the distinct demand for good, travel-oriented shots. He began to see that from a creative and financial point of view, it might pay for him to do extensive shootings in other countries for stock purposes. This way, he could travel and make a living from his photography at the same time.

Martin's technique for doing this stock travel work involves a considerable outlay of cash on his part, without any real guarantee that he'll see any monetary return. As with any stock agency, he's paid for the images that *sell,* not the ones that sit around in polyurethane sleeves, gathering dust.

The expenses he has to lay out are multi-faceted. First and fore-

**Black Star**
**450 Park Avenue South**
**New York, N.Y. 10016**
**(212) 679-3288**

Dear

Thank you very much for your inquiry about Black Star. We are a multi-service photographic agency. One of our activities is the sale of stock photography from our photographic library. In addition we carry out assignments for magazines here and abroad and we distribute individual pictures and picture stories throughout the world.

Through our stock library facility, we primarily sell individual photographs which are used by magazines, advertising agencies, a variety of commercial outlets, books, encyclopedia, etc. Black Star does not buy photographs. We work purely on a consignment and commission basis; the photographer receives 50% of each sale consummated when paid by the client.

Black Star maintains no formal contract with photographers submitting work for inclusion in the stock library. There is no minimum requirement for the number of years your pictures must be retained. We are not anxious, however, to take on material for a very short time, because the one thing this business requires is patience and one never knows when the calls will coincide with the subject matter you may have on file.

We have two specific requirements: 1.) Submission of work for consideration be accompanied by a self-addressed stamped envelope or a check to cover the cost of return and 2.) A signed waiver of responsibility which you will find enclosed.

Our interest these days is primarily color (35mm) although we do maintain an extensive black and white file. Pictures must have interesting subject matter, a strong center of interest, outstanding composition, be technically perfect, well composed and replete with visual impact. Experience shows that outstanding images sell----the rest just lie in the files in limbo.

Should you wish to make submissions, I assure you every courtesy and consideration.

Sincerely,

HC:jsa

Howard Chapnick
President

*Photographers who query Black Star with regard to placing material with the stock agency receive this letter in reply.*

most, he must hire the models he's going to take along on his "jaunts." They may or may not have that classic model "look," depending on the kind of photographs he's attempting to capture. He confers with stock agency executives to decide what look they are going for in the photographs to make them salable.

Once the models have been hired, Martin has to book planes, trains, hotels, transfers, and so forth to the various locations. Frequently, these trips involve stops in several places, so he has to have connecting reservations secured for everyone to be sure that his shoots go smoothly. Equipment-wise, he usually travels with a couple of cameras and a large quantity of film.

When Martin returns from his trips, he gets together with the stock agency to pick out the images which will go on permanent file. They try to select the ones that have the best chance of being sold, and the decision isn't always an easy one. Martin has done so much of this travel-type shooting nearly everything he comes back with has commercial potential.

An added benefit to this type of stock photography is the opportunity to meet people you would never meet under ordinary circumstances. For instance, when Martin was shooting Africa, he went to live with the natives in the bush. The people were warm and amiable, providing Martin with an unforgettable experience.

One final word about stock agencies. Before you sign with a stock agency do some comparison shopping. Not all agency contracts are the same. Some are tougher than others. For instance, Image Bank has a self-described "tough" contract, while other agencies are not as tough. Black Star, which is based in New York, will work with freelancers under a fiduciary responsibility to sell photographs and report those sales to the respective photographer. In fact, the president of the agency, Howard Chapnick, is one of the most respected men in the photography business. So remember, it pays to compare before you sign on the dotted line.

I would also add that you can make some very lucrative stock sales by selling stock photos for textbook illustrations. After all, textbook publishers have to get their pictures from someplace and frequently, they rely on the stock photo agency.

## BEING A GENERALIST

In the preceding pages, I've categorized the various types of photography that most professional photographers elect to do. In actuality, most professionals do more than one type of photography.

There are architectural photographers who also do still-life commercial work; photojournalists who make extra money shooting a public relations party; commercial photographers, like Bob Kiss, who also do editorial work. To restrict yourself to one category of photography, especially when you're starting out, is financial suicide.

Specialize in the area you're most interested in, and where you show the most talent. Don't limit yourself. Nearly every professional photographer I know does jobs for money, to pay the rent, food bills, and so forth. Once you've built up some money in the bank, you can be more choosy. But not at the beginning, and not at any time during your photographic career when you need the money.

Don't be a prima donna. It'll cost you.

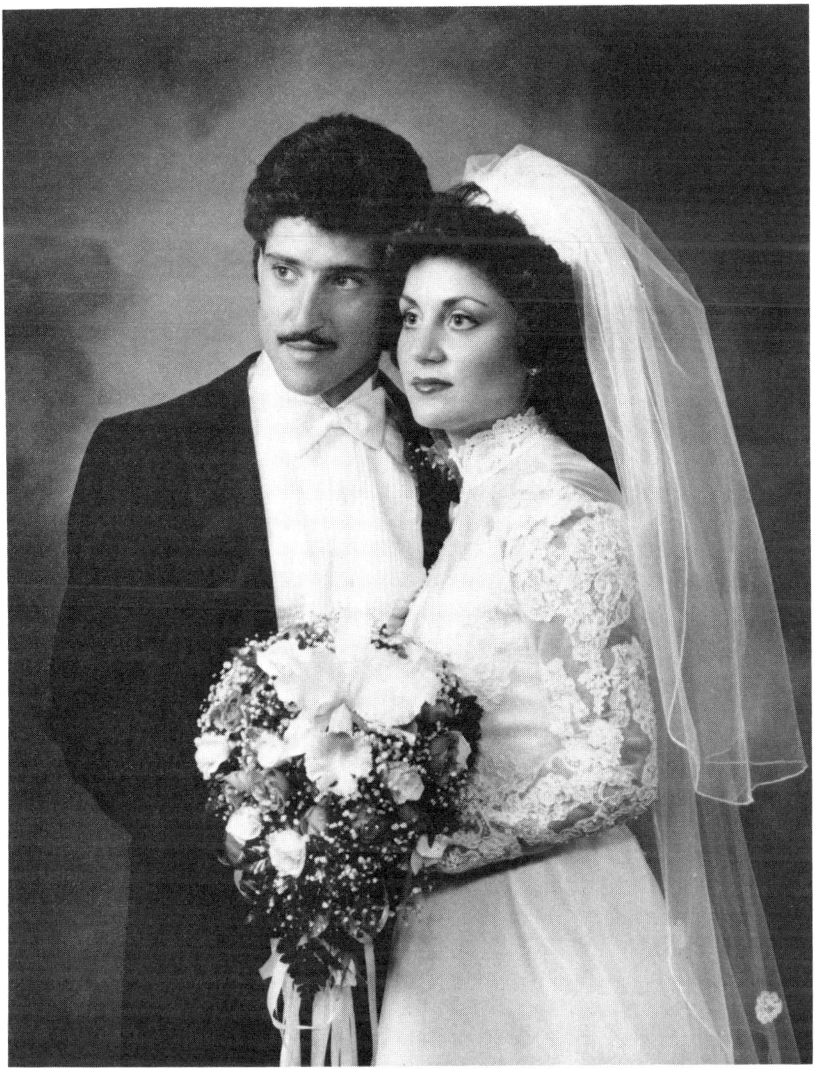

*This is an example of a formal studio portrait of the bride and groom. (Photo courtesy Dino Custom Color Photography, Elmhurst, New York)*

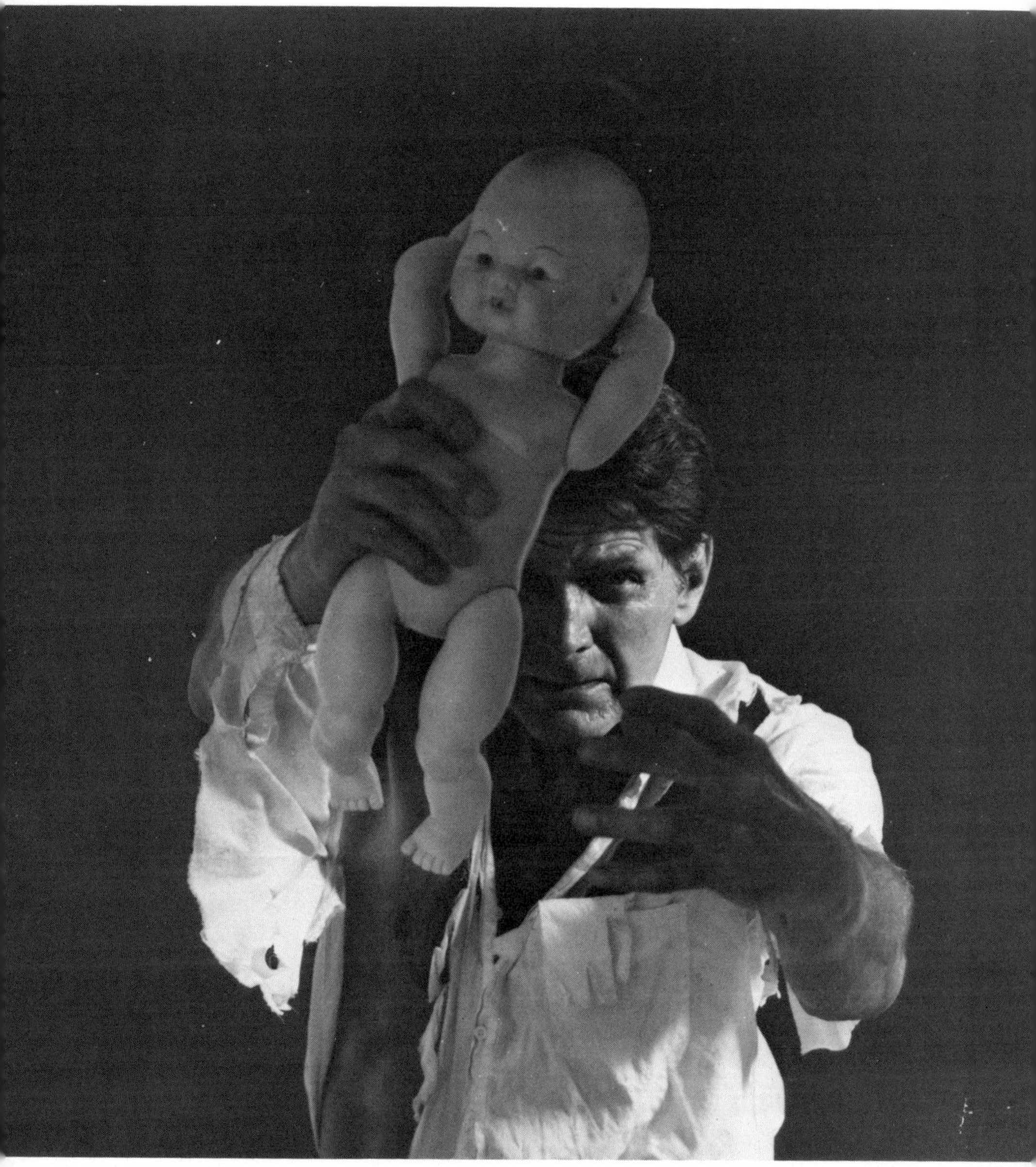

*This is one of the original photographs taken by Bob Osonitsch for a bookcover illustration. These shots are then used as rough models for the final finished illustration that an artist will create. (© Bob Larkin, 1984)*

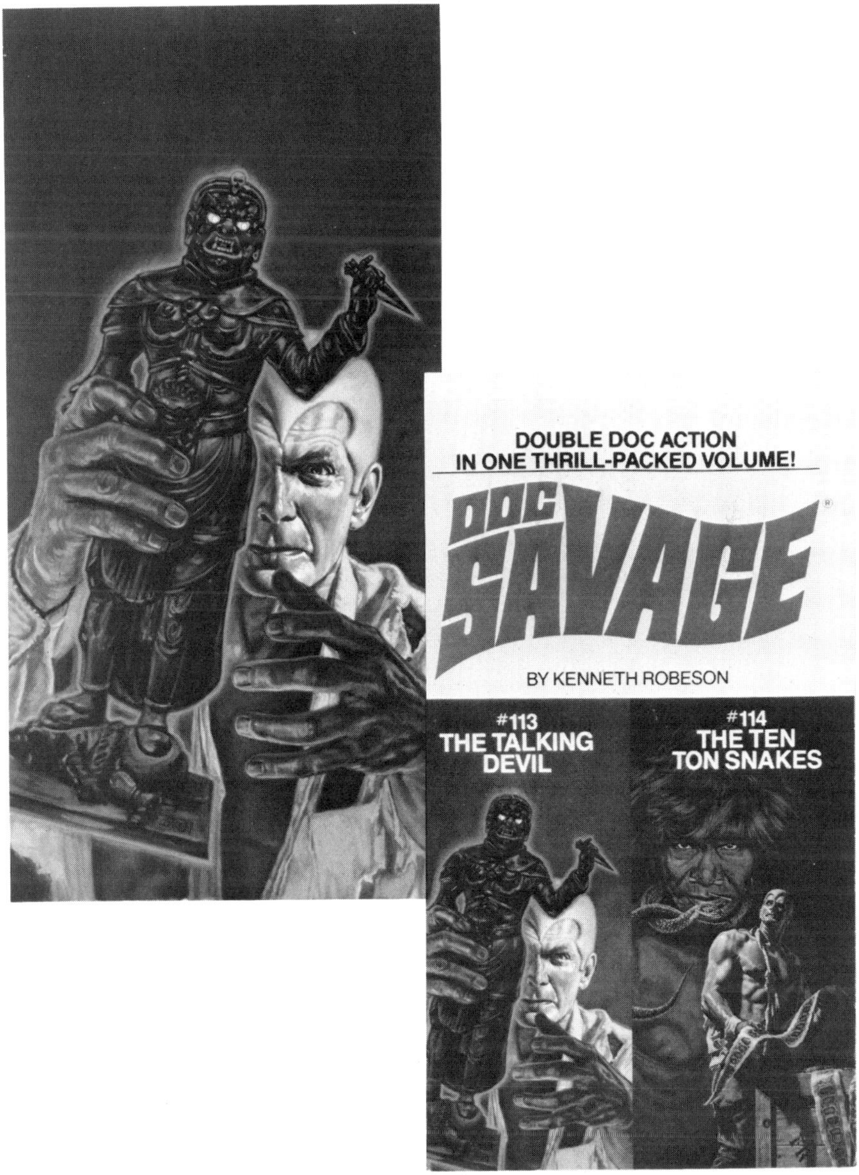


*Here's what the final bookcover painting looks like. The painting is by Bob Larkin, a fine artist who does bookcover paintings for Bantam and Avon books. In case you haven't recognized the subject of Mr. Larkin's painting, it's* Doc Savage, the Man of Bronze. *The painting appeared on the cover of one of the Doc Savage paperbacks. (© Bob Larkin, 1984. Jacket cover courtesy Bantam Books)*

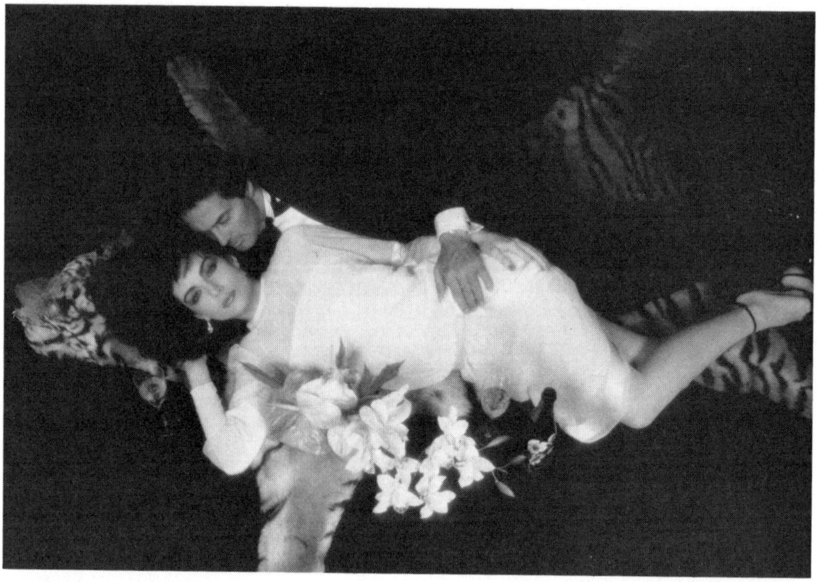

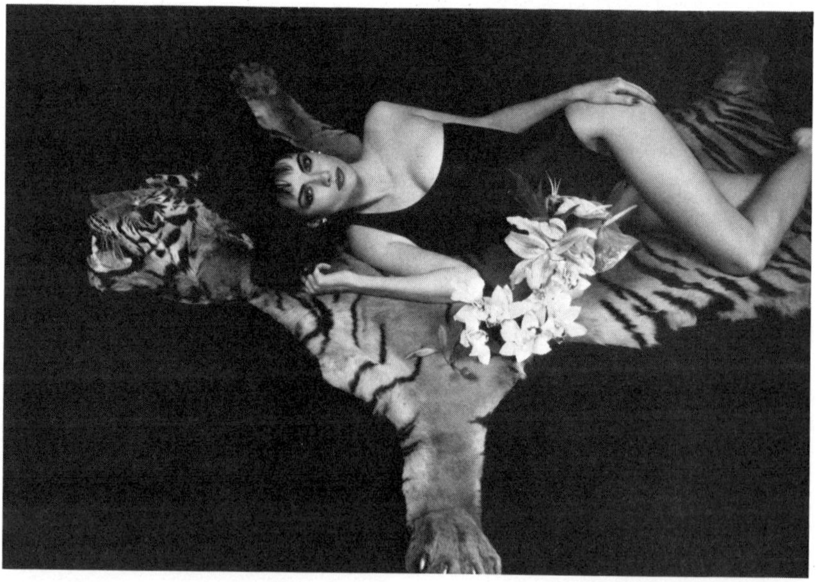

*These photographs were taken as part of a bookcover shoot. Each photograph has a different romantic slant. In the actual bookcover proof, you can see the direction that the art director felt would have the most appeal. (Photos © Don Banks, with special thanks to Ballantine Books)*

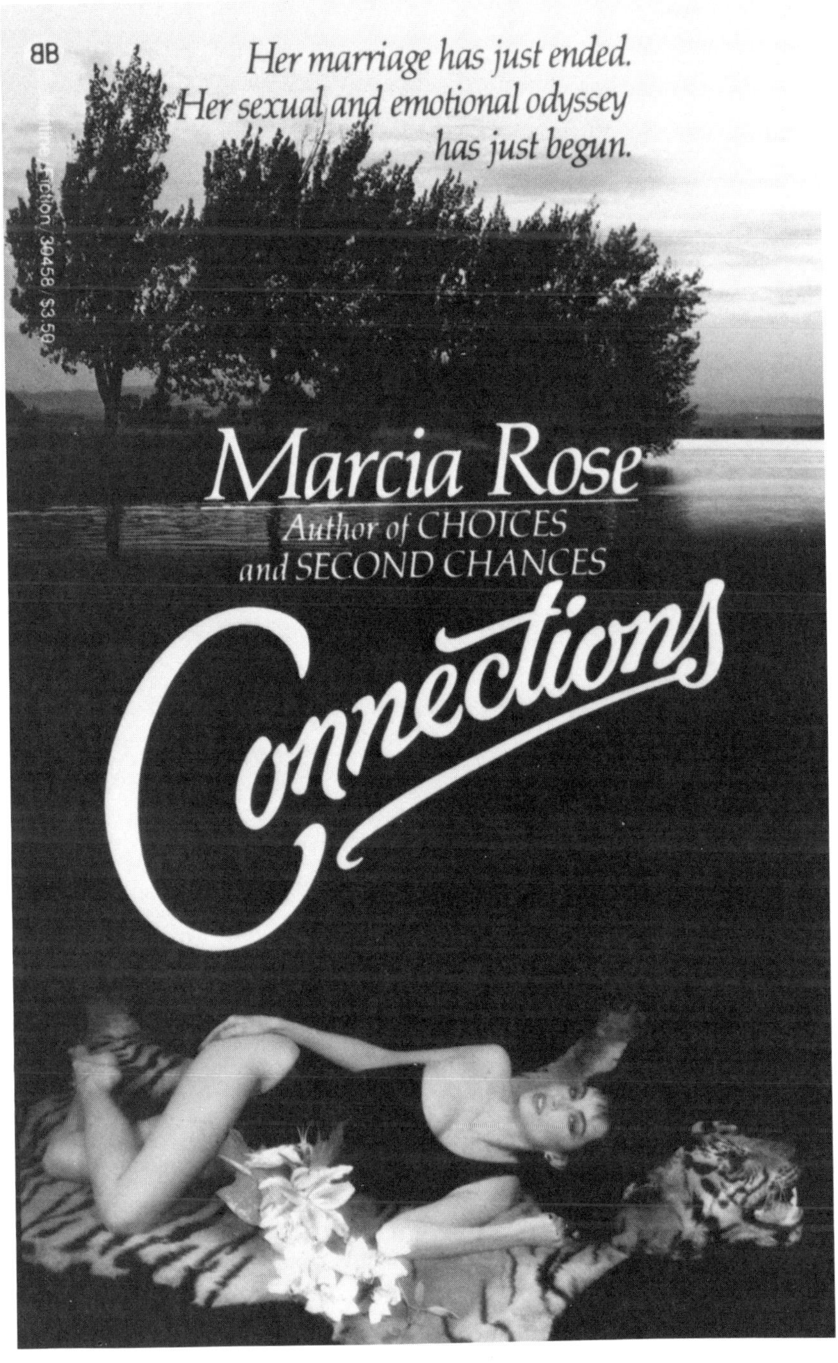
Her marriage has just ended.
Her sexual and emotional odyssey
has just begun.
Marcia Rose
Author of CHOICES
and SECOND CHANCES
Connections

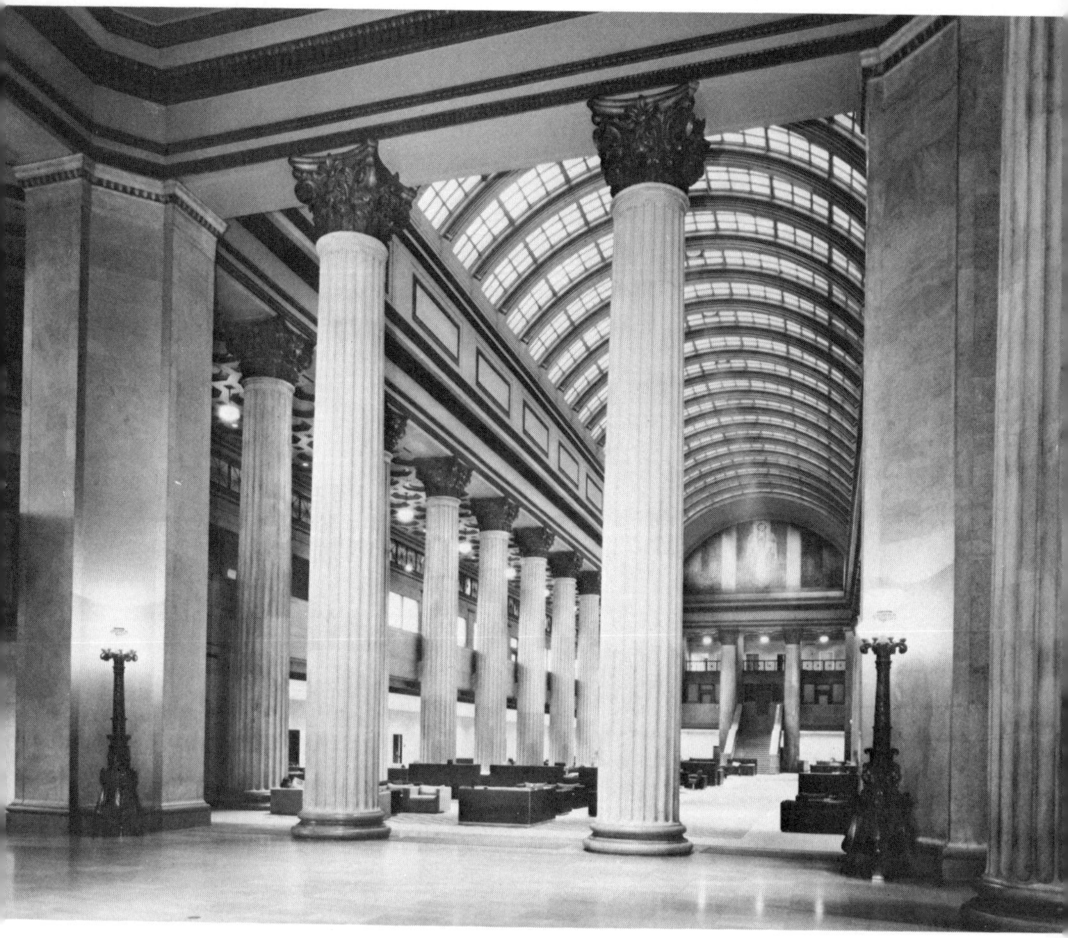

*This architectural interior photograph was taken of the Huntington Bank Restoration (formerly Union Commerce Bank) in Cleveland, Ohio. (Photo courtesy van Dijk, Johnson & Partners)*

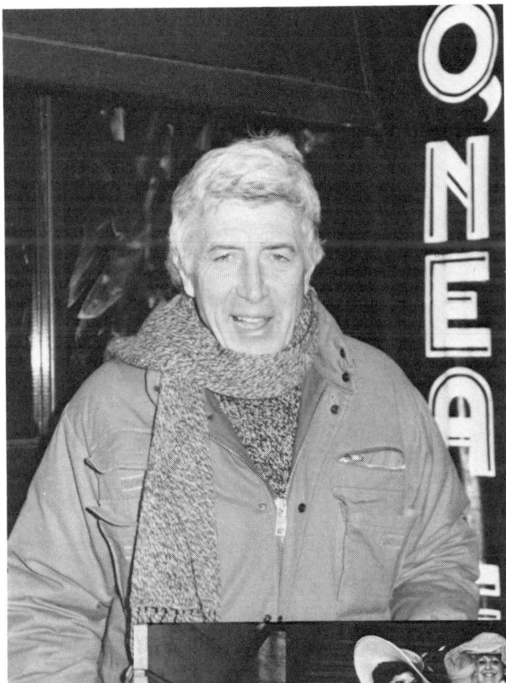

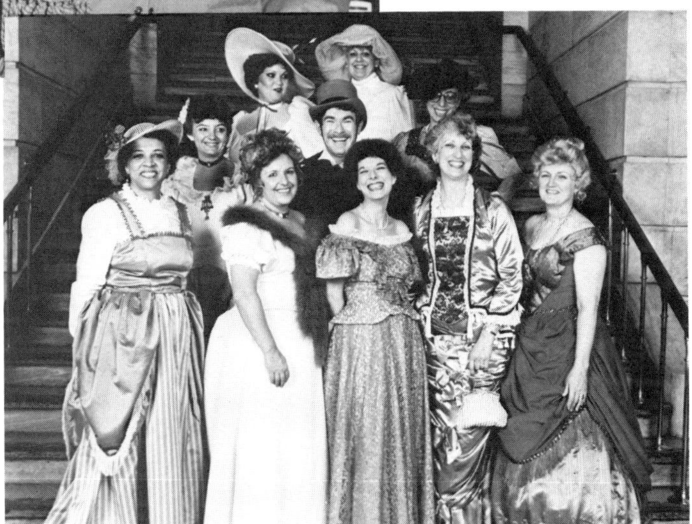

*(Top) This shot of a real gentleman, actor Patrick O'Neal, was taken for an article I did for* The Saturday Evening Post *magazine (Photo courtesy F.W. Rosen). The photograph at bottom was taken by Cathy Blaivas at a public relations function with a turn-of-the-century motif. It was subsequently used as part of a press release for* Engineering Information. *(Photo courtesy Cathy Blaivas)*

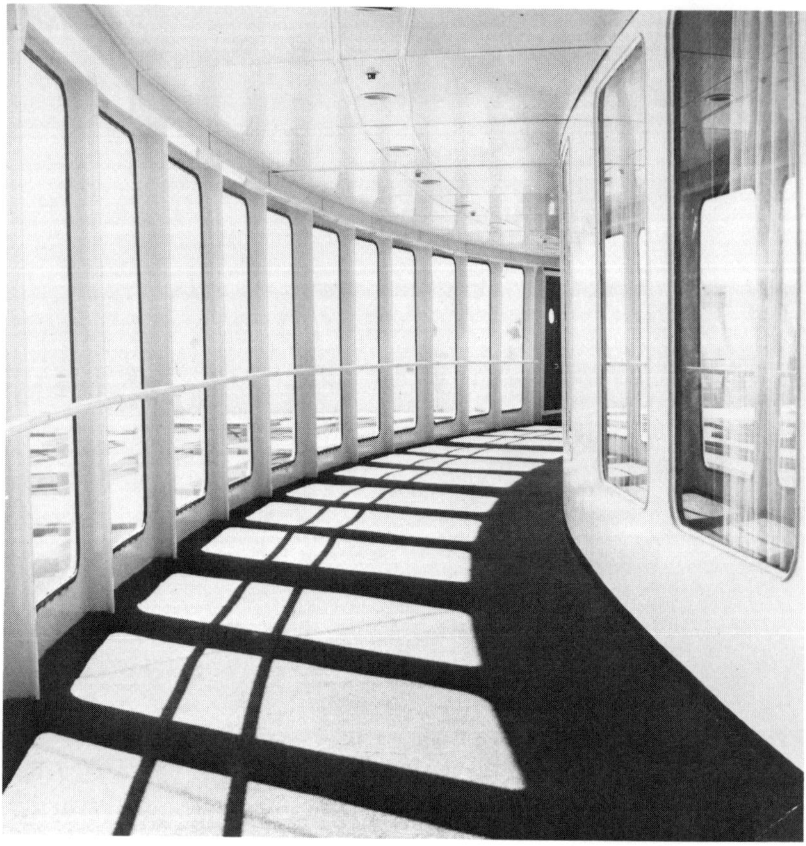

*Barry Winiker's cruiseship photography can also be sold as stock. Pictured is the upper deck of the cruiseship, Queen Elizabeth II. (Photo courtesy Barry Winiker, New York)*

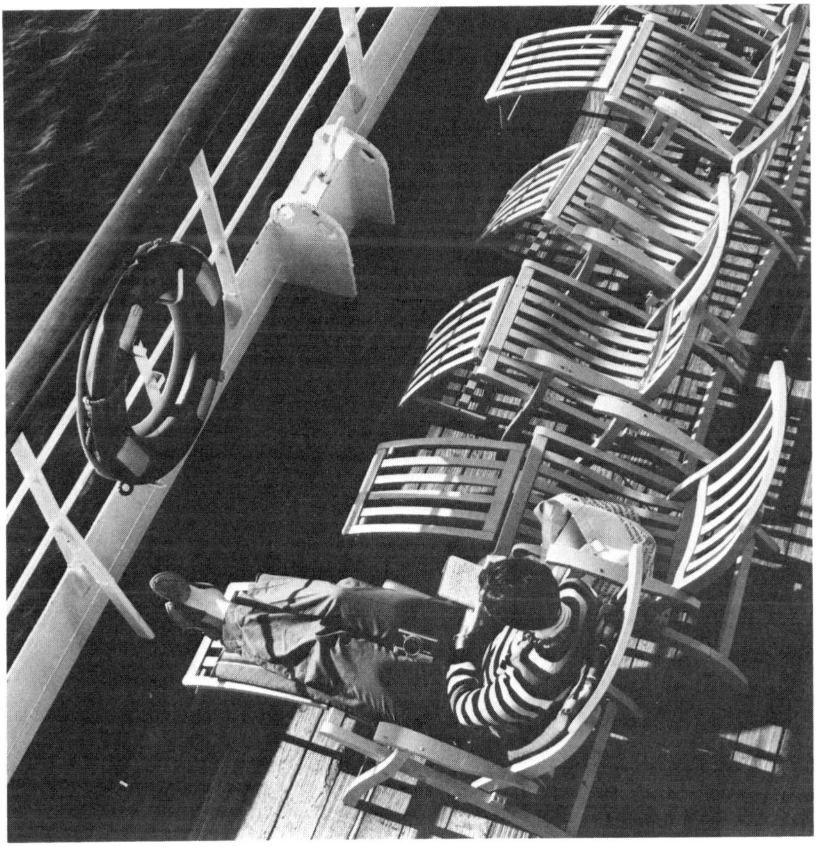

*Another of Winiker's cruiseship/stock photographs depicts a lone writer relaxing on a chaise lounge aboard the S.S. Rotterdam. (Photo courtesy Barry Winiker, New York)*

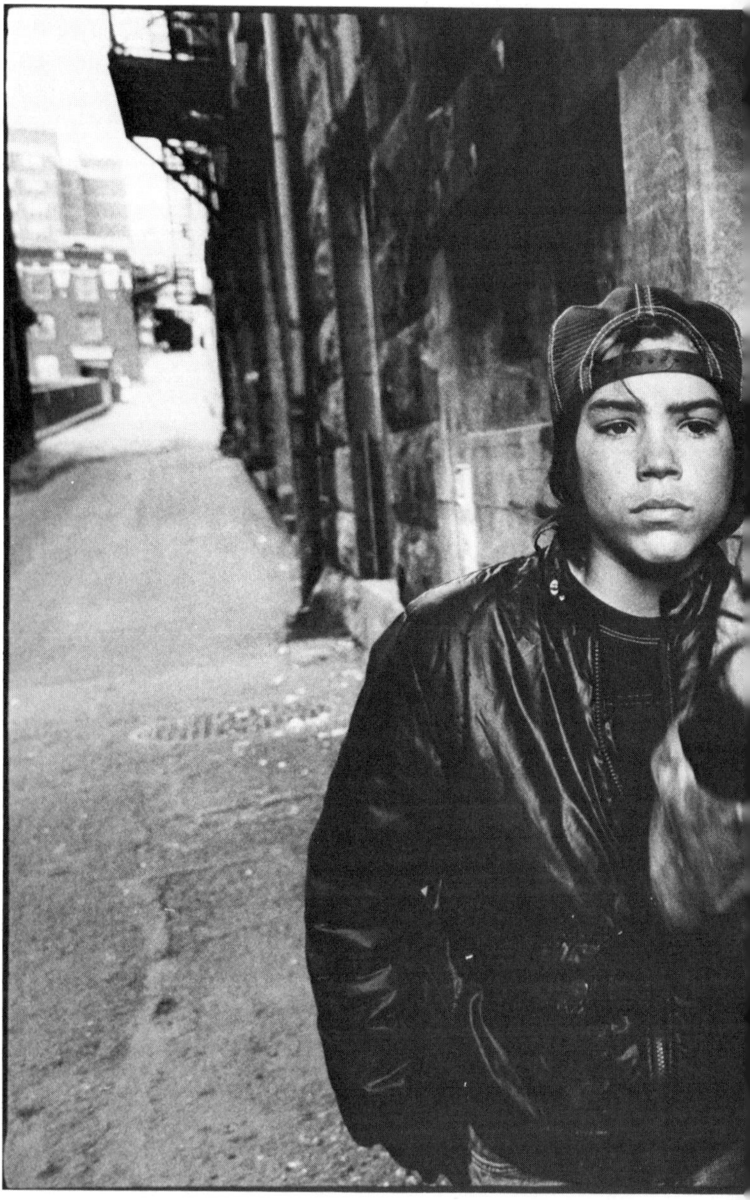

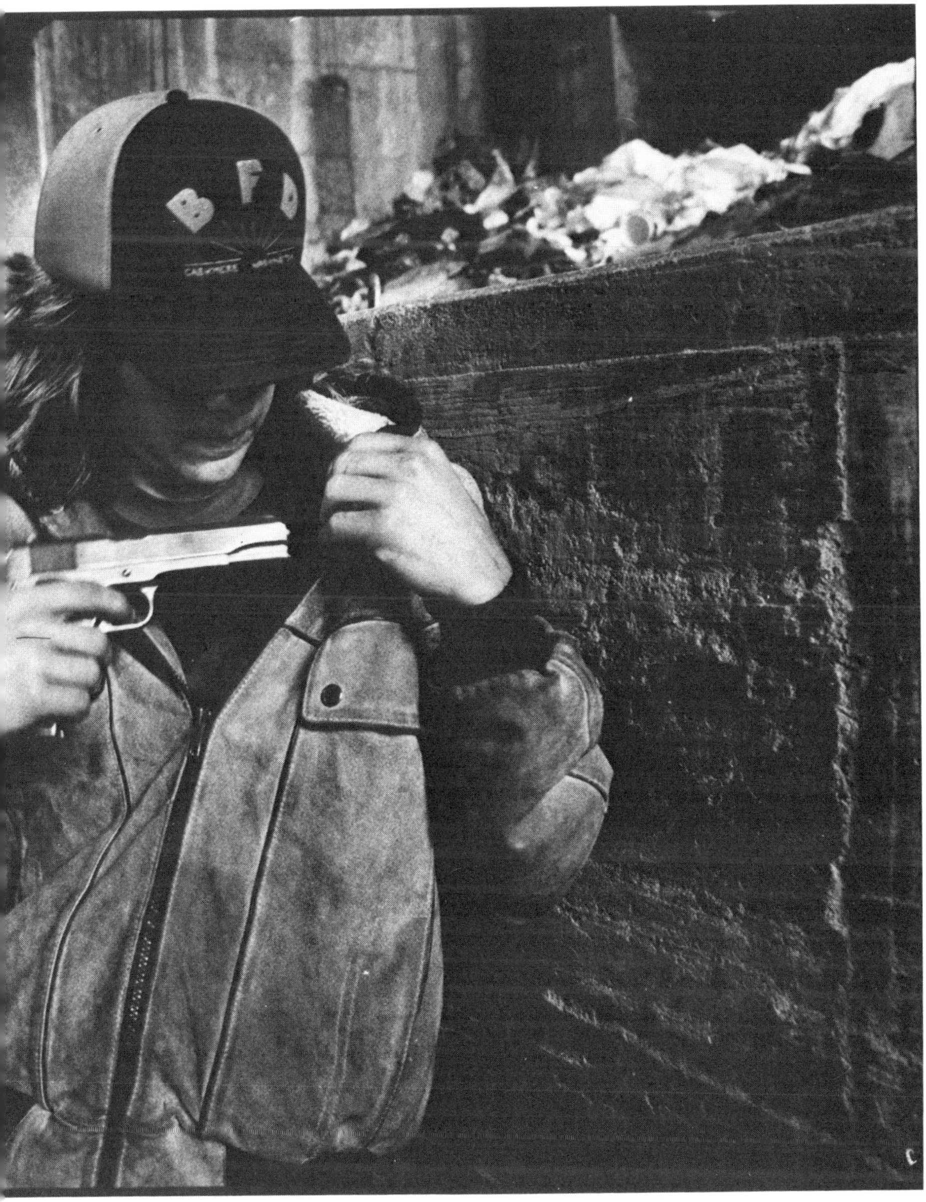


*Mary Ellen Mark won the University of Missouri School of Journalism—Canon Photo Essayist Award. This photograph was part of the winning essay which depicted street life in Seattle, Washington. (Photo courtesy Mary Ellen Mark)*

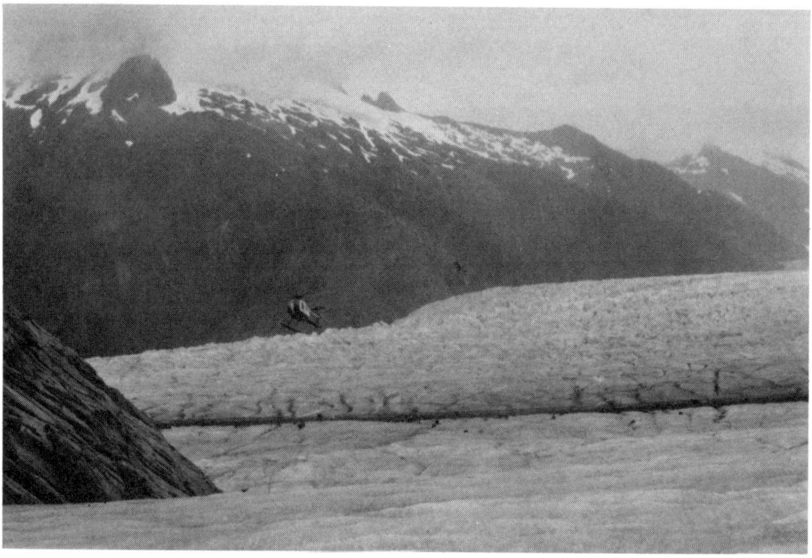

*Alaska's Mendenhall Glacier—a very cold place. (Photo courtesy F. W. Rosen)*

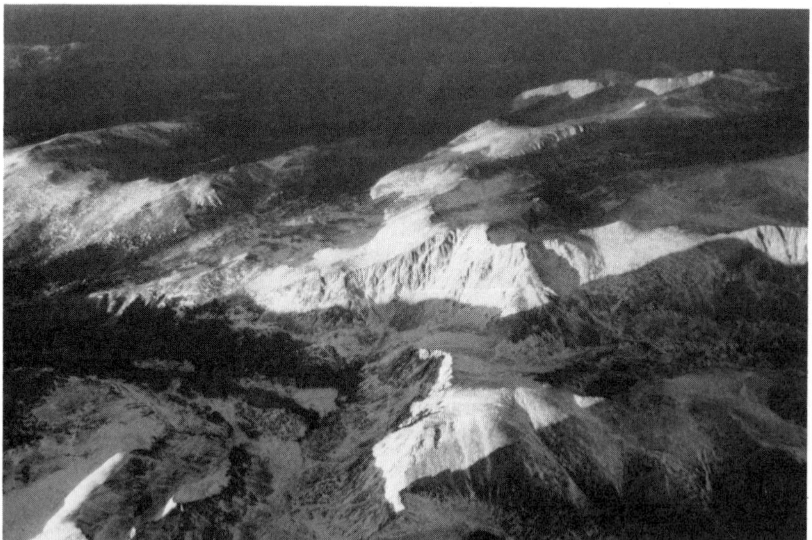

*Aerial shot taken for geographical purposes. (Photo courtesy Mara Bovsun)*

# CHAPTER THREE

# GETTING THE BACKGROUND

There are two basic options to becoming a full time photographer. The first option is to go into business immediately. If you've been shooting awhile and have the confidence, you may want to turn pro immediately. In that case, you can skip to the next chapter where I discuss how to get the money to finance your new business endeavor.

The second option is to get some experience before going into business. You can attend a school that specializes in teaching photography. There you'll get a lot of experience taking pictures. You'll be able to build up your technical abilities, your portfolio, and your confidence.

Another way to gain experience before going into business is to become a photographer's assistant. You work with the photographer in the studio and on location, doing everything from sweeping up after a shoot, to loading cameras, offering the photographer your advice, and sometimes, taking the actual shot.

Many beginning photographers like to go to a photography school and then become a photographer's assistant for a time, getting more experience and building up business contacts. You have to decide which options to select based upon your own personal and professional strengths and weaknesses.

## CHOOSING AN EDUCATIONAL PROGRAM

If you elect to go to photography school first, you're going to have to choose the type of program to enter. There are two general approaches to the teaching of photography. A professionally-oriented program prepares students to produce images that meet the needs and specifications of a client. The idea here is on actual practice, not theory. A school with such a photography program is interested in turning out professional photographers, not artists. In some schools with this type of program, a job counseling and placement service is also offered. But more often than not, you're going to have to get jobs on your own.

A fine arts program emphasizes the aesthetic. In such a program, the student is encouraged to develop his own personal artistic, vision, irrespective of meeting the requirements of a client.

Without hesitation, I'd recommend a professional program. It is useful to learn aesthetics, and a good professional program will include courses on aesthetics. To enroll in a fine arts program dismisses the reality of being a professional photographer: pleasing yourself with your photographs, and *then* your client. Except for museums and galleries, the fine arts photographer has a very limited market for his photographs.

I once interviewed the head of the photography program at a major, private university for a consumer photography magazine. He was a very kindly gentleman, who kept emphasizing during our interview that the coursework leaned heavy toward the fine arts and aesthetics. In fact, he was a fine arts photographer himself, who had had exhibits in many galleries, including the Light Gallery in New York.

When I asked him what his students did after graduation, he said that many of them opened their own studios. When I asked the professor how his students got their financing, he confessed that most of them came from families that financed them. They didn't have to worry about making a living. And the professor himself, I surmised, was making the bulk of his income from being a photography professor, *not* from being a professional photographer. Subsequently, the article about this photography school didn't run. The reason: the editor told me that he couldn't recommend, in an article, a photography school that turned out photographers who were unable to make a living without support from their parents. That would be a disservice to the reader. I agreed.

*What kind of college?* When selecting a photography program, you're also going to have to choose between going to a two-year or a four-year school.

Your prime consideration in attending any school is to get a well-rounded education. More than one successful photographer has told me that a well-educated photographer, because of his perspective, is better capable of creating interesting images.

The four-year schools will give you a better, overall education than the two-year ones. The other thing you should be aware of is that it's sometimes difficult to transfer credits from a two-year to a four-year school. So, should you decide to attend a two-year school, (and there are some good ones) make sure that at a later date, if you decide to transfer credits to a four-year school, you can. At the risk of sounding repetitive, I can't overemphasize the importance of education. It opens doors—especially the creative ones in your mind.

## EVALUATING COLLEGES

Today, attending college costs a lot of money. Some schools charge hundreds of dollars a credit and for a 128 credit Bachelor of Fine Arts degree. That can amount to a lot of money even before room and board and other miscellaneous expenses are included.

In addition, photography programs require the additional expense of equipment and supplies. So, before committing to attend a school for the sole purpose of studying photography, find out the following:

• Does the photography department supply camera, film, and lenses, or do you have to buy or rent everything on your own?

• Is the school you're really interested in attending what you are looking for? A college catalog doesn't tell you everything about the school so a visit would be wise.

• Check out housing, transportation to the school, cost of living in the area, access to major transportation arteries, which will be important should you have job interviews and/or want to go to galleries, museums, and so forth.

When you visit a school, ask the students who are already attending what they think of the photography degree program. Then, go to see the department chairman, not a secretary, and tell him you're thinking of applying, but want to know what the record of placement of graduates is as professional photographers. Be direct. It's your money and career on the line, not the department chairman's.

As a case in point, I attended the University of Southern California—as I mentioned earlier—and got my Master of Fine Arts in Film Production. I had visited the University of Wisconsin, Temple University in Philadelphia, and Indiana University to check out their film programs. I found them all lacking as far as professionally-oriented studies were concerned. I decided to attend U.S.C. when I realized it had the most professionally-oriented program in the country at that time even though the catalogs of the other three schools made them look very enticing.

*Which school should I choose?* Dr. C. Thomas Horrell, of the Department of Cinema and Photography, Southern Illinois University, surveyed 1043 educational institutions in this country that offer courses not only in photography, but in the graphic arts, and film as well.

The results of Dr. Horrell's survey of colleges offering coursework in all these subject areas is offered in Kodak publication T-17, entitled "A Survey: College Instruction in Photography," copyrighted in 1983. In fact, Dr. Horrell compiled his survey especially for Kodak.

This publication, which I urge you to write for, costs $4.95 plus $2.00 postage and handling, and is available from the Eastman Kodak Company, 343 State Street, Rochester, New York 14650.

For your more immediate information, with Kodak's permission, I've excerpted the data from the survey that is especially relevant. My criteria for inclusion in this list is that the schools listed have an appreciable amount of undergraduate hours in the following areas: basic photography, photojournalism, portrait photography, commercial photography, photographic illustration, industrial photography, the history of photography and color photography. As you can see, I'm choosing schools more on the basis of a practical rather than a theoretical approach to photography.

I am not using graduate programs as a requirement for inclusion in this chart because a good, undergraduate program should be enough to get you started in photography. Many people choose not to get their Masters degree in the area of their undergraduate major. They also might not have the money to do it either.

1. Brooks Institute, 2190 Alston Road, Santa Barbara, California 93108
Brooks offers 36 hours in basic photography, 12 hours in photojour-

nalism, 30 hours in portrait photography, 30 hours in commercial photography, 30 hours in photographic illustration, 30 hours in industrial photography, and 24 hours in color photography.

2. City College of San Francisco, 50 Phelan Avenue, San Francisco, California 94112.
C.C.S.F. offers 13 hours in basic photography, 8 hours in photojournalism, 6 hours in portrait photography, 13 hours in commercial photography, 8 hours in photographic illustration, 6 hours in the history of photography, and 12 hours in color photography.

3. Palomar College, 1140 West Mission Road, San Marcos, California 92069
Palomar offers 9 hours in basic photography, 9 hours in photojornalism, 9 hours in portrait photography, 9 hours in commercial photography, 15 hours in the history of photography, and 15 hours in color photography.

4. Santa Ana College, 17th and Bristol, Santa Ana, California 92706
Santa Ana offers 3 hours in basic photography, 10 hours in photojournalism, 13 hours in portrait photography, 3 hours in commercial photography, 3 hours in photographic illustration, 3 hours in industrial photography, 3 hours in the history of photography, and 9 hours in color photography.

5. Colorado Institute of Art, 200 East Ninth Avenue, Denver, Colorado 80203
C.I.A. offers 15 hours in basic photography, 6 hours in photojournalism, 6 hours in portrait photography, 12 hours in commercial photography, 6 hours in photographic illustration, 3 hours in industrial photography, 3 hours in the history of photography, and 9 hours in color photography.

6. Colorado Mountain College, Spring Valley, 3000 Road 114, Glenwood Springs, California 81601
C.M.C., Spring Valley, offers 16 hours in basic photography, 8 hours in photojournalism, 12 hours in portrait photography, 16 hours in commercial photography, 7 hours in photo illustration, 4 hours in industrial photography, 4 hours in the history of photography, and 29 hours in color photography. (By the way, for triviaphiles, Glenwood Springs is the final resting place of one Dr. John Holliday, better known as Doc Holliday.)

7. Colorado Mountain College, Timberline Camous, 901 Highway 24, Leadville, Colorado 80461
C.M.C., Timberline offers 9 hours in basic photography, 2 hours in photojournalism, 2 hours in portrait photography, 2 hours in commercial photography, 5 hours in photo illustration, 2 hours in the history of photography, and 9 hours in color photography.

8. Art Institute of Atlanta, 3376 Peachtree Road, N.E., Atlanta, Georgia 30326
The Art Institute of Atlanta offers 17 hours in basic photography, 5 hours in photojournalism, 5 hours in portrait photography, 23 hours in commercial photography, 5 hours in photographic illustration, 2 hours in industrial photography, 1 hour in the history of photography, and 9 hours in color photography.

9. Illinois State University, Normal, Illinois 61761
I.S.U. offers 21 hours in basic photography, 6 hours in photojournalism, 6 hours in commercial photography, 3 hours in photographic illustration, 3 hours in industrial photography, 9 hours in the history of photography, and 6 hours in color photography.

10. Southern Illinois University, Carbondale, Carbondale, Illinois 62901
S.I.U., Carbondale offers 16 hours in basic photography, 6 hours in photojournalism, 3 hours in portrait photography, 3 hours in photographic illustration, 3 hours in industrial photography, 6 hours in the history of photography and 19 hours in color photography.

11. Indiana Vocational Technical College, 3501 First Avenue, Evansville, Indiana 47710
I.V.T.C., Evansville offers 16 hours in basic photography, 2 hours in photojournalism, 6 hours in portrait photography, 11 hours in commercial photography, 3 hours in photographic illustration, 14 hours in industrial photography, and 8 hours in color photography.

12. Indiana Vocational Technical College, 646 Franklin Street, Columbus, Indiana 47201
I.V.T.C., Columbus offers 8 hours in basic photography, 4 hours in photojournalism, 8 hours in portrait photography, 23 hours in commercial photography, 13 hours in photographic illustration, 17 hours in industrial photography, and 9 hours in color photography.

13. Indiana Vocational Technical College—Northcentral, 1534 West Sample Street, South Bend, Indiana 46619
I.V.T.C., Northcentral offers 9 hours in basic photography, 3 hours in photojournalism, 8 hours in portrait photography, 15 hours in commercial photography, 15 hours in photographic illustration, 15 hours in industrial photography, and 12 hours in color photography.

14. Hawkeye Institute of Technology, 1501 East Orange Road, P.O. Box 8015, Waterloo, Iowa 50704
Hawkeye, named after a famous Korean War surgeon, offers 11 hours in basic photography, 14 hours in photojournalism, 19 hours in portrait photography, 14 hours in commercial photography, 3 hours in photographic illustration, 14 hours in industrial photography, and 9 hours in color photography.

15. Center For Creative Studies, 245 East Kirby, Detroit, Michigan 48202
The Center offers 6 hours in basic photography, 3 hours in photojournalism, 1 hour in portrait photography, 27 hours in commercial photography, 6 hours in photographic illustration, 6 hours in the history of photography, and 6 hours in color photography.

16. Grand Valley State Colleges, Allendale, Michigan 49404
Grand Valley offers 19 hours in basic photography, 9 hours in photojournalism, 6 hours in commercial photography, 9 hours in photographic illustration, 3 hours in industrial photography, 6 hours in the history of photography, and 40 hours in color photography.

17. Lansing Community College, 419 N. Capitol, Lansing, Michigan 48901
Lansing offers 14 hours in basic photography, 8 hours in photojournalism, 9 hours in portrait photography, 8 hours in commercial photography, 3 hours in photographic illustration, 5 hours in the history of photography, and 11 hours in color photography.

18. Rochester Institute of Technology, One Lomb Memorial Drive, Rochester, New York 14623
R.I.T. offers 56 hours in basic photography, 18 hours in photojournalism, 9 hours in portrait photography, 9 hours in commercial photography, 33 hours in photographic illustration, 12 hours in industrial photography, 7 hours in the history of photography, and 15 hours in color photography.

19. Randolph Technical College, 629 Industrial Park Avenue, P.O. Box 1009, Asheboro, North Carolina 27203
R.T.C. offers 11 hours in basic photography, 12 hours in photojournalism, 12 hours in portrait photography, 12 hours in commercial photography, 8 hours in photographic illustration, 5 hours in industrial photography, and 3 hours in the history of photography.

20. Ohio Institute of Photography, 2029 Edgefield Road, Dayton, Ohio 45439
O.I.P. offers 13 hours in basic photography, 3 hours in photojournalism, 18 hours in portrait photography, 18 hours in commercial photography, 18 hours in photographic illustration, 7 hours in industrial photography, 3 hours in the history of photography, and 12 hours in color photography.

21. Art Institute of Pittsburgh, 526 Penn Avenue, Pittsburgh, Pennsylvania 15222
A.I.P. offers 15 hours in basic photography, 8 hours in photojournalism, 8 hours in portrait photography, 11 hours in commercial photography, 8 hours in photographic illustration, 4 hours in industrial photography, 4 hours in the history of photography, and 15 hours in color photography.

22. Austin Community College, P.O. Box 2285, Austin, Texas 78768
Austin offers 13 hours in basic photography, 33 hours in portrait photography, 32 hours in commercial photography, 5 hours in photographic illustration, and 65 hours in color photography.

23. Texas Christian University, Fort Worth, Texas 76129
Texas Christian offers 12 hours in basic photography, 18 hours in photojournalism, 6 hours in portrait photography, 9 hours in commercial photography, 9 hours in photographic illustration, 3 hours in industrial photography, 3 hours in the history of photography, and 12 hours in color photography.

24. Northern Virginia Community College, Alexandria Campus, 3001 N. Beauregard Street, Alexandria, Virginia 22311
Northwest offers 33 hours in basic photography, 2 hours in photojournalism, 2 hours in portrait photography, 15 hours in commercial photography, 2 hours in industrial photography, 19 hours in the history of photography, and 7 hours in color photography.

25. Clover Park Vocational Technical Institute, 4500 Steilacoom Boulevard, S.W., Tacoma, Washington 98499
Clover Park offers 19 hours in basic photography, 5 hours in photojournalism, 6 hours in portrait photography, 19 hours in commercial photography, 3 hours in photographic illustration, 1 hour in industrial photography, 1 hour in the history of photography, and 62 hours in color photography.

26. Ryerson Polytechnical Institute, 50 Gould Street, Toronto, Ontario, Canada M5B 1E8
Ryerson offers 30 hours in basic photography, 8 hours in photojournalism, 9 hours in portrait photography, 9 hours in commercial photography, 9 hours in photographic illustration, 12 hours in industrial photography, 8 hours in the history of photography, and 33 hours in color photography.

*Which are the best?* Among professional photographers I've spoken with, two names always come up as the best photography schools in the country: R.I.T. in New York and Brooks in California. Those schools are cited as giving the student the most well-rounded education in photography.

Before moving on, let me point out that the reputation of a program in a particular school is frequently behind the times. Someone can be recommending a school on the basis of their experiences at that school 5 years ago, when, in fact, the school's reputation has gone downhill since that time. That's why it's important to check out a school thoroughly before committing yourself to go there.

Whichever school you eventually decide to attend, make sure that it is a legitimate educational institution with a reputable background.

## THE PHOTOGRAPHER'S ASSISTANT

What's it like to gain experience by working as a photographer's assistant? Two years ago, I interviewed a number of assistants in the hopes of getting an answer to the question. Some of the answers they gave were rather surprising.

"We had to patrol New York City, looking for guys who'd pose nude for *Playgirl* magazine. The art director just walks up to good-looking guys on Park Avenue and asks if they'd like to pose. I'm carrying all the boxes of equipment and the photographer is standing there with his camera and the tripod and she goes up to some guy and asks if we could take his picture for a test shot. Well, 90 percent of the guys say drop dead, but some say yes."

The fellow carrying the boxes is Vince Guarneri. He's an R.I.T. graduate and a full-fledged photographer's assistant. When he was going to school he had no idea he'd be carrying boxes and sweeping floors before a photographer would even let him *touch* a camera.

At no time did any instructor say to Vince you'll have to assist. He simply thought he'd go out there and be a photographer. It didn't quite happen that way.

Vince graduated, and armed with a super-technical background, came back to his native New York City, where he got a job (through family contacts) at a local lab. There, he learned photographic printing, but soon became as he puts it, "too smart for the owners. They didn't want me around and I left."

After a stint as a technical sales assistant for a photographic company, a friend of his who was an assistant saved him from following what might have been a boring technical road.

"My friend," Vince recalled, "said, 'Why not get into assisting and get back into photography?' He introduced me to a few people and I started working for photographers at $40 a day.

"You start at $40 'til you learn the ropes. Basically, you're just standing there, sweeping the floor, loading cameras, getting coffee, just being around. After you do that for awhile, you get up to the $50–$60 level, where you're doing a bit more coordinating—working with clients, booking models—and getting more on-camera experience. Then, you move onto the level I call the 'final plateau,' just before going out on your own, the $70–$80 bracket, which is where I'm at now. That's where the photographer calls *you* in to save the shot: 'How do I light this? Help me do the shot.' I've worked for guys who didn't know a yellow and magenta filter don't make red. At this level, I'm doing exactly what the photographer does or working directly with him. We'll come up with answers for problems together."

"Together" seems to be a key word in assisting. Kathryn Millan, another assistant working in New York, emphasized compatibility when I interviewed her in 1982. She said it was important to get along with the photographer and the other people in the studio.

"Every studio has a different way of doing things. I worked with a really good still-life photographer. I learned how to do the fancy frosting of bottles; you know, when you make that Coke bottle look ice cold, dripping with water vapor. Then I worked with a fashion photographer and he had to shoot a model holding an ice-cold bottle. He didn't know how to ice the bottle, so I showed him the trick the still-life photographer used."

Kathryn studied photography at the University of Texas and graduated with a BFA in art. It was while studying fine arts that she got hooked on photography and decided to pursue it.

After spending a year in Abilene doing her own shooting, taking photo illustration courses and teaching photography in the public school system, she decided to come to New York to be a photo illustrator. It was a move well thought out.

Before leaving Abilene, she'd come to Manhattan with her portfolio from her photo illustration class. She met with photographers to get their reaction and establish contacts. Their comments were so positive that when she went back to Abilene she began saving money for her move to New York in the spring of 1981.

Immediately, she checked in with ASMP for suggestions on getting assistant jobs. She was talking to the receptionist there when a photographer happened to call to say he needed an assistant.

"There was my first day of assisting right there. I took that as a good omen. I only worked that one day with him, but it took the tension out." After that, she did the typical knocking on doors so many young professionals seeking jobs have to do in Manhattan, using ASMP and *Black Book* listings to find jobs. "I put together a resume and printed it up. A lot of studios ask to see resumes before they'll hire you."

At the first couple of studios she was low on the totem pole among other assistants. She ran for lunch, ran for props the stylist forgot, ran to the bank for the photographer, doing, as she puts it, ". . . all the things behind the scene that need to be done to get the shot together."

She got some jobs simply because a photographer was going on location and needed an extra pair of hands to load and unload vans and carry equipment. Being a woman has never posed a problem, though, because "*nobody* carries anything that's too heavy."

Kathryn figured it would be two years before she could go out on her own and get agency clients. Along the way, she picked up small jobs, like shooting composites for rock bands, to make ends meet.

One thing Kathryn regretted was not having more of a technical background. Still, she was picking up experience in the studio. "A studio manager invited me over to the studio one afternoon when nothing was going on and took out a Polaroid back, showed me how to load it and said, 'Close your eyes, sit here and practice.' It was wonderful."

One photographer's assistant who did have a heavy technical background when he came to New York was Dan Forte. Much of Dan's experience was acquired as a Navy photographer.

"Whenever the Navy had a big assignment, they sent out four people on a motion picture and a still photographer. I was the still photographer."

Dan had joined the Navy to get further photography experience after graduating Orange Coast College in California with a photography degree. Attending ASMP meetings in Los Angeles, he'd realized how far he had to go before he could be a really good photographer. Without enough money to attend a photography school, the Navy was the answer. They trained him to be a photographer, but there was a period during his enlistment when he was just an assistant for the Navy, too.

"The first year I did a lot of compartment cleaning and watchstanding and stuff that didn't have anything to do with photography. After almost a year, I was allowed to shoot training exercises on my own and my stuff was so good that I got more assignments."

After his hitch was up, Dan went to Arts Center College in Pasadena and then decided that "the big stuff was in New York and that's where I was going." Here Dan's experience departs from the norm for assistants. In 1982, after being in New York for only eight months, he was about ready to go out on his own.

"My first contacts were by letter, while I was still in Los Angeles. I came to New York between semesters and showed my book to photographers and asked for their input." He was able to see 25 or 30 photographers this way and told them he'd be back. When he came to New York in December 1981, he had contacted the people he wanted to work with—photo illustrators—and got on with them right away.

Dan began to get his own clients through personal contacts. A roommate in Los Angeles had a cousin who was an art director at an ad agency who introduced him to other agency people. A friend in New York who was doing a lot of editorial work helped, too. He told Dan, "Look, don't assist. Here are some names. Go out and contact these people." Dan did and began doing editorial work.

By December 1982, he was looking to break out on his own. He and some friends had been looking for studio space. But until he could secure enough clients, he kept assisting at $75 a day. And some of his assignments bordered on the dramatic.

"There were some ads running for Fruit-of-the-Loom that I assisted on. We had to shoot these wildcats, a jaguar and a mountain lion, and one was supposed to be on the model's shoulder. We had to build a platform for the cat to sit on behind the model. Well, the cat was five times bigger than we expected, and we had to take down the platform, right there in front of the client, and make a bigger one, put it up and get guy wires down in about 15 minutes. We were on tight time."

*An update.* Since I spoke with these assistants two years ago, the life of an assistant has not changed much. If anything, the people interviewed downplayed the financial and emotional insecurities they had to put up with as assistants.

I have heard stories from more than one reliable source about famous commercial photographers who pay their assistants next to nothing for their services. One even feels he's such a great photographer, his assistants should just be honored to be working for him, let alone paid for the "privilege."

In short, this is ridiculous. You may make $40 a day when you're starting out, but don't let anyone con you into taking an assistant's job for the experience because you don't need the "experience" of not being able to pay your bills.

Remember, your time is valuable and you should be paid for it regardless of the level of your experience. Don't be intimidated by a photographer's reputation. He's not paying your bills, you are. If you have ever tried to be creative when you have monetary pressures hanging over your head, you'll understand why it's better to drive a truck than to work at something you love and not get paid for it.

As to the people interviewed for the article, what are they doing now, two years later? Well, as soon as the article was published Dan Forte moved back to the West Coast to form his own photography business. What about Vince and Kathryn, the two other assistants?

"I only assist on special occasions now, for $100 a day and only for former clients," Vince Guarneri told me. In between mainstream assisting jobs, Vince has picked up a permanent client.

"I work for Whaledent International, as a medical and dental photographer," he continues. "I'm on a retainer to shoot dental operations and presentations. I also photograph for public relations firms."

Why didn't Vince proceed into the photographic mainstream and take the next step, which for him would have been becoming a commercial photographer?

"I decided not to go out and hit the streets. There are too many people out there. Right now, my overhead is low, I make good money and I have time to build my own portfolio with photography I shoot for myself."

He adds that eventually he wants to be more established as a medical photographer, and that his business is completely computerized.

Kathryn Millan has been busy too.

"I'm still assisting for a really nice photographer, who lets me use his equipment to do my own jobs on the side," Kathryn says.

"I photograph interiors on assignment, as well as parties and benefits. And I am making more money than two years ago."

In her three years of assisting, how has the reality of becoming a pro been reconciled with her initial expectations?

"It seems to be a little harder than I thought to become a pro. When I do go out on my own, which is at least a year away, I'm going to have to get a loan to put things together."

One assistant who did form his own business is Chad Weckler. He provides further insight into the life of a photographer's assistant and the transition to full-time photographer.

"The average assistant," Weckler says, "assists five years before going out on his own. During that time span, he'll probably work three to four days a week, at an average of $75 per day. Even if the assistant makes a maximum of $15,000 a year, that's still not a lot of money, especially when you take into consideration the heavy cost of equipment."

It was one year ago that Weckler decided to go out on his own and become a photographer. He found the experience emotionally and financially devastating. He's now saving up, from assistant's jobs, to go independent again. Why did he fail the last time out?

"I wasn't totally prepared," he says. He elaborates;

"I didn't have enough money when I went into business and gradually, my confidence was worn down." He felt broken.

"To be successful as a photographer, you have to have some sort of financial security and more importantly, the confidence that you'll succeed. Without that, all the money in the world isn't going to do you very much good."

Weckler points out that today, there are more people assisting than ever before. Many novice assistants are commanding the same fees as experienced assistants making it that much tougher for the experienced ones to be paid what they're worth. I asked Weckler why some assistants make it and others—with seemingly everything going for them, including talent, money, and contacts—don't make it.

"If I had the answer to that question," he answered laughing, "I'd probably be rich!" (I hope he makes it.)

*The reality of assisting.* How many assistants eventually become full-time, working, professional photographers? No one knows.

It is true, though, that assistants are exposed to a variety of experiences, everything from technical problem-solving during a shot, to the proper way to communicate with a client. But the question remains: should you become an assistant *before* going on your own?

There's no definitive answer. One can be derived, however, by asking yourself these three questions:

1. How experienced am I, technically and in dealing with people?
2. How easy is it for me to raise the money to go into business?
3. How will I get the contacts for jobs?

If you have the experience from any source—school, the Armed Forces, or some other places—you may be wasting your time assisting. You'd fortify your case to go independent if you have or can raise the capital to do it.

In contrast, if you don't have enough experience, and most importantly, if you're not absolutely certain that you'll make it, then you're better off going the assistants route. You can try to become an independent at a later date.

## CHAPTER FOUR

# ARRANGING YOUR PORTFOLIO

Last night, someone referred me for a job. When the client called to discuss the job with me, he hadn't gotten final approval to hire me. He did, however, know what my credits were. I managed to sell him further on my abilities over the phone during our initial conversation. When he called back a short time later, he had received final approval from his superior to contract for my services.

After I finish typing this chapter, I'm going to put on my good suit, dress shirt and tie with the brontosaurus design from the Museum of Natural History. Then I'm going to take the subway into the City, to discuss this job with him. But despite my credits and my suit, and especially my jazzy tie, I'm fully aware that no matter how well I do on this job, I might never get another one from him. Why? Because I won't have my portfolio with me.

My portfolio contains published articles and photographs. Unfortunately, I'm in the process of revising it, and the portfolio is in total disarray. So, when I speak to the client, I'm going to have to give him xerox's and slides of my work which is not nearly as impressive or as professional as showing him my portfolio.

While the client may know me by referral and reputation, he may also know others in the same way. The one thing that would distinguish me from everyone else is a portfolio that shows the range of my capabilities. Nothing can substitute for it and help to get you work in the long run—not even a big mouth.

## THE PURPOSE

The portfolio is your basic selling tool. It contains the images that you think are best representative of your talents and abilities.

You can put your portfolio together either while you're attending a photography school, or during the time you put in as a photographic assistant. Chances are, you'll be adding and deleting from your portfolio, as your photographic skills improve.

The specific purpose of a portfolio, quite simply, is to sell a potential client on your ability to do the job they have in mind. The portfolio should reflect your artistic and technical competence, and your ability to sell a product with your photographs. Regardless of the fact that he has never hired you, the portfolio has to convince the potential client that *you* are the one to shoot the job he has in mind, and that he should hire you, and not someone else.

## GENERALIZED PORTFOLIO

Depending on the area of photography that you're specializing in, you're going to need a portfolio that reflects the type of images taken in each category of photography.

If you're going to be working in a number of different areas—commercial, editorial, and corporate—your portfolio should have a selection of photographs for each category.

You might set it up by beginning with your strongest shots. For this example, let's say they are color slides of work in the editorial area. The first twenty-five slides would be your best work in editorial. You should then include one or two transitional pictures before getting to the second set of twenty-five, which are in the corporate annual report area. Follow with one or two transitional slides again, then finish up with your best twenty-five slides in the commercial area.

You may also include tearsheets from any published work. Arrange them by photographic category in a binder, once again with transitional shots, this time prints, between each category.

When putting together this type of portfolio, remember that the idea is to show the potential client your photographic versatility. The shots you use should be varied, but of the same uniformly high quality.

## A SPECIALIZED PORTFOLIO

In addition to your generalized portfolio, you may also want to build a portfolio that specifically covers each of the photographic categories you work in. If you specialize in one category in particular, you may only want one portfolio in that category.

*The wedding portfolio.* Wedding and portrait photographers don't usually use binders and slides in trays to exhibit their work to prospective clients. What they do is show a prospective client a number of different wedding albums. The idea is to show the different types of shots, in the different types of albums, because the wedding photographer is not only selling his photographs, he's selling the albums as well.

In the wedding album, there'll be different types of formal (posed), ceremony, and reception shots. While the ceremony and reception shots rarely change (except for the use of special effects, like double exposure) there has been a trend in recent years to use environmental portraits as part of the formal shots.

Some more enterprising wedding photographers are taking the time and effort to take the wedding party down to a local scenic spot, like a park, where the beautiful, natural setting reflects back upon the momentous life occasion that's about to take place. These are environmental portraits.

In addition to showing the client the sample wedding album, some wedding photographers like to also take propsective clients into a separate room in their studio where they've set up a slide projector. Here they will show slides that illustrate the different types of wedding shots.

*The corporate portfolio.* The corporate portfolio should contain images shot for annual reports and brochures as well as aerial and architectural shots that are non-editorial.

In some ways, the photographer doing corporate work is going to be the most versatile. One day he may be shooting a shopping center from the air for a real estate development company. The next day, he's out shooting for an annual report in a factory. And the day after, he's been hired to shoot a building that houses telecommunications devices for the phone company.

Because of the wide variety of images, the corporate portfolio will contain considerably more than 40 slides. Slides are usually shot for annual report work. A tray containing 80 slides makes a good form of presentation.

Within those 80 images, try to show your range from "no nonsense" portraits shot for an annual report, to artistic architectural images of a building that wound up in one of the company's brochures sent to customers.

In addition, arrange the tray so six to eight consecutive photographs show how a specific assignment was covered. Also, to provide the viewer with an idea of what you are like, include some of your own work that conveys to the viewer a personal look at familiar objects like trees, signs, the beach—just about whatever interests you that you'd like to shoot more frequently, if you had the time and money.

In addition to your slide tray, your presentation will be enhanced by a separate binder of tearsheets, if you have them, and one or two really good annual reports and brochures that you shot. Just make sure that you only put in your good work. If you have any doubt about including a shot, a brochure, or an annual report that contains work you are not proud of, better to leave it out.

Some additional advice for putting together your portfolio comes from Virginia Murphy-Hamill. She's the director of magazine design for Hearst Business Communications. Her background includes art direction for pamphlets, booklets, and annual reports. She also works as a freelance art director.

"As far as what would turn me off in a portfolio, almost nothing except sloppiness. It might be nice if a photographer has slides in his portfolio to bring a portable light box or a small slide viewer with him, to facilitate viewing.

"I also like to see specialized shots, like something using a special effect. This distinguishes one photographer from another."

*The editorial portfolio.* As to the content of the editorial portfolio, include work in the following categories: photojournalism, editorial illustration, and architecture (done for magazines). You may want to put each category of work in separate mounts or separate sleeves. For instance, if you take along 36 slides in mounts, the first group of 12 would be photojournalistic shots, the second group of 12 would be editorial shots and the third group of 12 would be architectural in nature. Or, you can mix them up, if you believe it makes a more graphically attractive presentation.

What do the professionals look for in an editorial portfolio? "What I do is ask the photographer to send in either tearsheets of his published work or slides. It's all right to send the slides in sleeves. As a matter-of-fact, it's more impressive to me if a photographer has his slides in sleeves because then I don't have to go through unwieldy boxes," says Pat Perry. Perry is the associate editor of *The Saturday Evening Post* magazine. He is responsible for bringing all of the photographic work for the magazine.

"I look for photographic competency," Perry continues. "I like to see images in a number of different photographic formats, so I know the photographer is not limited. That way, if I have an assignment that requires someone to shoot in large format, I'll have a photographer, who's portfolio I've seen who does shoot large format, who I can assign that job to. I can tell you that the really good photographers whose work I've seen work in different formats."

If you want to take Perry's advice a step further, mount your color slides in black mats. Slides mounted in black die-cut mats made out of cardboard help emphasize the colors of the slides more clearly because of the color contrast between the slides and the black mats.

If you then take along a loupe when you go into the editor's office, he can simply take the slides in their mounts, hold them up to the light, and look at them through the loupe. Be sure, though, that each mount is the same size. I like 11 × 14, though others prefer 8 × 10. Regardless of the size you choose, remember to keep them uniform throughout your presentation.

I would also suggest bringing along, in a separate binder, prints of your black-and-white work. Few photographers today are really proficient in black-and-white photography, and editors like to see some proficiency in that area.

There's also another reason to emphasize black-and-white work. Usually, the color pages in a magazine are limited. While it is possible to convert color slides to black-and-white pictures for a magazine, you lose detail and contrast in the resulting photograph. The editor is a lot better off assigning the "shoot" to a photographer who can shoot some good black-and-white images.

As to how many total images you should present, I wouldn't go over forty. That's enough for an editor to judge your ability. But among the forty, include some of your personal, as well as professional work. It'll give the editor an insight into your talent.

*The commercial portfolio.* The commercial portfolio could contain images from the following photographic categories: fashion, advertising, catalog, and bookcover.

Notice that I am combining a number of different photographic categories under the commercial banner. The reason behind this arrangement is that in each of these areas you are essentially selling or promoting a product. Whether it be a high fashion gown, a bottle of expensive perfume, a new toy, or a best-selling book, it is still commercial in nature. In all cases, a product is being shown to the public to attract their attention. All of the photographs from these categories can be combined in one portfolio, or, if you wish, you can make up a separate portfolio for each, assuming you have enough shots in each category.

Lyman Gaylord, an account supervisor in public relations for The Rowland Company, gets to see many a commercial photographer's portfolio because his client is Canon. Gaylord screens many of the photographers who want to build a business relationship with that large camera and lens manufacturer. His advice about setting up your portfolio:

"Forget slides," Gaylord says. "What am I supposed to do? Hold them up to the light? It's better to bring along prints. I'd say no more than 25 but no less than 15 because I find that most portfolios are overstocked.

"I'd like to see a range of subject matter in the photographer's portfolio, unless I'm looking for a specific type of shot."

How about black-and-white shots?

"I like to see black-and-white very much," Gaylord continues. "Aside from a separate promotion the vast bulk of photos we send to newspapers are going to be black and white because that's all most papers publish. So be sure to include black-and-white prints in your portfolio. And be sure to leave behind something, like an 8½ × 11 print, so the potential client will remember you. It's more impressive than a business card.

Gaylord's advice about taking along prints, mounted in a binder, is well-taken. Prints give the person looking at them a long, relaxed opportunity for scrutiny. With slides, you always have to do something to see them–set up a projector, or hold them up to the light.

In the commercial portfolio, I would also include tearsheets of any published work, in a separate section. This, of course, establishes your credibility as a photographic salesman.

*The videocassette portfolio.* With the increasing use of videocassette recorders as a playback device, photographers with a little bit of daring are experimenting with portfolios on videocassette.

They take slides that best exemplify their work and transfer them to videotape. Special visual effects, like fades and dissolves are added with music synchronized to match the effects. Camera moves, like dolly and trucking shots, may also be added to heighten the visual imagery. Music is also synced to these camera moves too. Add in effective, versatile framing including close-ups, medium shots, and long shots, and you wind up with a dynamic presentation.

If you decide to have a video portfolio created for you, (and I recommend strongly that you go to a video studio or store to do it), make sure that your slides are transferred onto ½″ VHS videotape of uniformly high quality, like TDK's Super Avilyn. There's little difference visually between VHS and Beta (some video pros claim Beta is better), but VHS is the most popular taping format. I've also been in very few agencies that didn't have ½″ VHS equipment.

Avoid like the plague the new, untried ¼″ format. There's even less of a marketplace with ¼″ equipment. By the way, be sure to call ahead before the interview and ask the art director at the agency if he does have a ½″ VCR. It'd be rather embarrassing if you show up with your brand new videocassette with nothing to show it on.

## PORTFOLIO MATERIALS

Zippered portfolios that hold prints and tearsheets in sleeves come in a variety of sizes and materials. Sizes range from 8 × 10 to 20 × 24. The materials forming the outer covering may be made from real leather, imitation leatherette, or even fabric.

If you buy a zippered portfolio, test it out a couple of times before buying it. It should zip easily. The last thing you need is to worry about the zipper breaking. Also, make sure the portfolio is not too big for you to carry it around. If you're making a number of stops on a typical afternoon, you shouldn't have to worry if you'll fit through an office building's revolving door with your portfolio.

Another type of portfolio you may want to consider buying is a box, covered with one of the materials I've mentioned above. Boxes are good for carrying laminated tearsheets, mounted transparencies, and large prints.

If your portfolio is a tray of slides, don't use the box the carousel comes in. It's tacky to arrive at a client's doorstep with a box that has emblazoned in bold letters with a maker's logo. What happens if the job is to do a shoot for Fuji and the carousel box you have is marked Kodak?

Buy a carousel tray box without any lettering on it. There are some attractive ones available that come in black, blue, and red.

## CATCH-22

No, this isn't a plug for Joseph Heller's book. But a catch-22 does exist when you're putting your portfolio together. If the portfolio is to contain the professional work you've done, what do you do if you've just gone into business and haven't done any professional work yet? And what do you do if the type of photography you want to do requires the use of models, but you don't have the money to hire any to take shots specifically for your portfolio?

Let's address the first question first. If you haven't got any professional work done on assignment to put into your portfolio, you're going to have to shoot work that *looks* like it was done on assignment. In other words, you should deliberately set out to imitate a certain style of photograph that in your particular photographic category, sells the product.

The point is take a look at photography, fashion, and other magazines to find out what kind of images you're going to have to include in your portfolio to convince an art director to give you a job. Use the photos you see as a jumping off point for your own creativity.

Now to the second question: How do you get models to pose for nothing? It's not very difficult. Models have portfolios, just like photographers. When they are first starting out, and even later, when they need different shots for a revised portfolio, they will trade the photographer their time, in return for some of the pictures from the "shoot." This type of shoot is called a test.

To get a model for the test, contact one of the modeling agencies in your area, tell them you're testing, and you need a model. They'll usually send some models down to your studio for a "go see,"—you look at the model and decide if she'd fit into the picture you have in mind. Once your selection is made, just set up a time for the "shoot" that's mutually convenient.

If you don't have modeling agencies in your geographic area, you might have to advertise in a local paper for models. Of course, you could get everyone from bored housewives to nubile high school cheerleaders applying. Choose the person you think will look good on camera, is easy to talk to, and can at least move fluidly like a model without being self-conscious.

## SOME GENERAL ADVICE

Steve Pollock is the genial and perceptive features editor of *Popular Photography* magazine. He's probably seen thousands of portfolios in his job, in all of the different photographic categories I've just discussed. He has some general portfolio advice for the professional photographer.

"The most important, single thing is if I'm pleasantly surprised by a photographer's portfolio. I can tell you that doesn't happen very often," says Pollock, casting a laconic glance at his perpetually overcrowded desk.

"In general terms, the portfolio should be of consistently high quality. Ruthlessly edited. Weak pictures suggest that the photographer doesn't know the difference between a strong shot and a weak one.

"Another thing I like to look for is a linking theme between shots. The shots should all hang together, making it easy to sift through." Pollock pauses.

"The pictures have to make it simply as pictures, without an explanation. The technical quality should be high, the exposures sharp and the printing of consistently highest quality."

"As far as I'm concerned, anything that makes my looking at pictures an easy task is okay. I don't care if the photographs are in a neat looseleaf binder or a fancy leather portfolio. I just want them to be good and I don't want to have to fight to take them out of the wrapping.

"As far as submitting a portfolio to *Popular Photography* is concerned, the photographer should bear in mind that the photographs will have to lend themselves to a magazine layout. The photographer should also include a self-addressed stamped envelope with return postage so the portfolio can be returned without any trouble. It also suggests that someone doesn't care enough about his work if they don't put their name and address on their slides.

"It helps too if the photographer sends a cover letter with the photographs that clearly explains what he intends with the shots. It's nice if the person writes and can express himself." Continuing to deal with his magazine's requirements, Pollock explains:

"People send prints larger than 11 × 14. Why? There's no point. They're hard to handle and they'll be reduced anyway if we use them in the magazine. I also ask photographers to send slides in a carousel or in slide sheets and that prints shouldn't be mounted because that makes them big and bulky."

In general, Pollock advises photographers to send him two slide sheets. "Forty slides are plenty," he told me. "People send 100 or more and similar shots of the same image. Pick the best one and include that one, not the others."

In conclusion, Pollock suggests that the photographer include a cover letter with contact information, so he can call or write the photographer if he's interested.

"We have a large backlog of photographs right now. Even good stuff doesn't get used." Which only means that the professional photographer should not take a first rejection from a magazine, or any client, as something personal. Rather, they should keep querying. Politely.

"There's this guy who's contacted me several times and he's shown me his portfolio. When I didn't use his shots, he insulted me. Several times."

"I guess you're not going to give him a layout," I responded.

Pollock shook his head, then glanced at the floor. I followed his gaze, and saw it.

There by Pollock's feet was the "chip" that the rude photographer had knocked off his shoulder all by himself. All he had to be was nice, and he would have at least had a chance.

# CHAPTER FIVE

# FINANCING AND ESTABLISHING YOUR BUSINESS

Now comes the moment of truth. After weighing all the options, after countless conversations with your loved ones and friends about whether to go into business or not, you decide to take courage in hand and plunge in. You're going to form your own photography business. You have the experience, the education, the sheer nerve necessary to say, "I know the odds are against me, but I have to try!"

Brave words, and if you can't support them with hard cash, you're done before you start. Now you need to evaluate the options available to finance a new photography business.

## RELATIVES

The most obvious source of financing is your relatives, for two reasons. The first one is a basic business tenet: try to get someone else to invest their money, so you don't have to invest yours. The second reason is that your relatives may trust you to pay back an unsecured loan.

An unsecured loan is one given without collateral. Your only requirement is a moral one—I must pay back this loan because I am obligated to do so.

You can sign a legal agreement to pay the loan back, with interest, by a certain date should you so wish. Some people going into busines like to do this so they don't feel an emotional obligation. After all, it's tough to feel independent from your parents when they're financing you. A signed, notarized agreement makes everything nice and business-like, and your parents or a relative who is lending you the money will respect you that much more for this approach.

You shouldn't feel embarrassed to go to a relative for help, though. More than one famous photographer was initially financed by relatives. In short, if you have the opportunity to ask a relative for money, take it. The worst they can do is say no.

Realize that the amount of money you'll need will have to pay for establishing your business including necessary equipment, space, film processing, model fees, construction of a portfolio, and so forth. You have to be prepared, regardless of where you get your financing, to go for at least four months without a penny coming in. It will take that long to establish contacts, do some jobs on assignment, and eventually get paid for those assignments. You know, you don't get paid immediately. Usually, it takes thirty days before you see a check for your efforts.

## LOANS

Another way of financing your business is the bank loan. There are various types of loans that are available depending on your financial circumstances.

*Passbook loan.* If you have some cash in the bank, either in the form of a deposit in your bank passbook, a CD, money market, or IRA, then you can take out a loan. Generally, this is referred to as a passbook loan. When you take out a passbook loan, you are freezing the money in your account that you're making your loan on. In other words, you can't spend any of it until the loan is paid off.

To take out a passbook loan, you simply go down to the bank where you have your account. You tell a loan officer that you want to take out a loan for X amount of dollars, to be secured by the money in your account. The bank then loans you the money, which you agree to pay back with interest—whatever the prevailing interest rate is at the time.

You are then issued a payment book. A separate payment is forwarded to the bank over the period of time of the loan. For instance, if you borrow two thousand dollars at an interest rate of 15% per annum for three years, you will have 36 separate payments. This includes the interest and the principal averaged out over those 36 months. When the last payment is made, your collateral is unfrozen, and you're free to spend the money again.

The advantage of a passbook loan over many other types of loans is the knowledge that you always have the money in the bank to pay off your debt. It's relatively easy to get the bank to give you the loan, and your credit rating will escalate because banks love nothing more than loaning money to a person who consistently pays off. Remember, they make no money if you default, and they have to collect the principal. They make money on your monthly payments because payments include principal *and* interest.

*Loans with other collateral.* You can also take out loans with other forms of collateral. Collateral can be property, like houses, condominiums, automobiles, or boats; investments, like stocks and bonds; and life insurance policies that have a face value.

When taking out a loan with forms of collateral other than cash, the same procedure applies. The bank gives you the loan of the cash, which you pay back in regular monthly payments—with interest, of course.

There can sometimes be a problem getting this type of loan if the bank officer approving the loan is not sure he wants to accept your collateral. He may, for instance, reason that if you default, the bank shouldn't have to go to the trouble of selling a boat left as collateral. So your job when you initially go in for the loan is to convince the officer that your collateral can be liquidated quickly, and that you're a good credit risk.

*Loans without collateral.* I've rarely heard of a businessman in any field who got a loan without some sort of collateral. The bank wants to know there's something, no matter how small, that partially secures their investment.

Occasionally, a bank will grant a business loan on the basis of the bank officer's feelings that the person borrowing the money is a good credit risk. It's rare, but it happens. In general, though, it's good to have some sort of collateral before you even attempt to get a loan.

If you think you can get a loan with little or no collateral, your best bet is to apply at a commercial rather than a savings bank. Commercial banks are used to dealing with businessmen, and while the odds will still be against your getting the loan, they will come down a bit if you apply at the commercial bank rather than the savings bank.

## CREDIT CARDS

For the aspiring photographer a credit card can be a lifesaver. It's possible to have a credit limit ($5,000 or more is possible) on some credit cards. So, your monthly payment on a $5,000 bill might be approximately $200 on VISA or Mastercard. That's affordable, even though the 20% interest rate is very high.

Use a credit card as a last effort to establish your business. Remember that you're paying an outrageous amount of interest, and it could take years before a heavy credit card bill is paid. You have to be absolutely confident that you're going to have enough business to pay off the debt. Otherwise, the credit card company is going to get angry.

Some companies will eventually give the bill over to a collection agency. When they can't collect, they'll give it to a lawyer, who goes to court and gets a judgement against you. A short while later, you'll be at your bank, writing a check and expecting to cash it against the money in your account. Lo and behold, the teller tells you that someone has put a lien against your account. Your money is frozen until the debt is paid. Want to take a wild guess who froze your account? This scenario has happened to more than one professional photographer.

So, only use a credit card when you know you'll have the money to pay the debt back, or you're willing to pay the debt back over a period of time (which might even be years). Of course, you can also use a credit card if you don't mind the subsequent turmoil of living and doing business over your means. (I hope you won't choose the last option, because it really isn't one at all.)

## CREDIT UNIONS

Credit unions are actually banks conducted on cooperative principles, usually by an association of members of the same occupational group or of the same local community. For example, auto workers might belong to a credit union composed of other auto workers.

If you're currently in an occupation that has a credit union which you belong to, you may want to think about taking out a loan from the credit union to establish your photography business. With collateral, or with someone co-signing your loan who's also a member of the credit union, you can frequently borrow money at reasonable interest rates.

## THE LEGAL FORM OF YOUR BUSINESS

Once you've procured the money to start your business, the next step is to decide on the type of business, as a legal entity, you're going to form. You have a number of choices, and you should consider them carefully before committing to one or the other.

You should also realize that in addition to your own requirements, the Internal Revenue Service has theirs. They like to know what kind of business you've formed so they can then tax you accordingly. Unfortunately, there's no way to avoid them. Let me also say that in the last few years there have been a great many changes in the tax laws. What I am about to offer is *very general advice* for setting up your business. I urge you to consult an accountant or a tax lawyer before you make any decisions.

*Individual ownership.* The business you form can take one of three legal avenues. It can be individually owned. It can be a partnership, or you can elect to incorporate. Let's begin with individual ownership.

To form a business based upon individual ownership, you do nothing. Let's say you plan to become a professional photographer, which you finally do. At the beginning of your new career, you've decided not to work in partnership with anyone. All you do is select the place of business (loft, home, or office), get the money to buy the equipment, and you're in business as an individual owner. It's not even necessary to file any special legal papers. The government doesn't require it. By the way, a business that's individually owned is also referred to legally as a sole proprietorship. The terms are interchangeable, and you may call your business one or the other.

*Partnership: General or Limited.* More friendships have been ruined because two enterprising individuals, who also happened to be friends, decided to go into partnership with each other. Since partnership can involve working closely on a day-to-day basis, even friends can get on each other's nerves. There is also the possibility of having your "friend" make business decisions involving large amounts of capital without your knowing about it until it's too late.

If I sound cynical, I am. As a businessman, you can trust no one but yourself, and I say this from my own personal experiences. So, to protect yourself, whenever entering into a partnership agreement, be sure to get it on paper. Have the agreement looked over by a lawyer, and then notarized once all of the terms have been mutually agreed upon by you and your partner.

There are two kinds of partnerships you can form: the general partnership and the limited partnership. When you form a general partnership, either or both parties contribute money to form the business. Sometimes, one party may contribute money, while the other contributes his business and technical expertise. But regardless of who contributes what, in a general partnership, each partner has an equal say in how the business operates when he contributes 50 percent of the capital or 50 percent of the business expertise. Now, here's the problem with this sort of business agreement.

Since each partner has an equal say in how the business operates, one partner can enter into a business agreement with a third party without the other partner being aware of it. Yet his partner, who's still ignorant of this new agreement, is bound to it anyway. Now, let me give you a hypothetical business situation with hypothetical partners to illustrate this point.

Supposing Partner A (Adam) has to go out of town on business, personal or otherwise. The important thing is he's away. Now Partner B (Bart), an agressive sort, commits to shoot the interior of a large, midtown Manhattan hotel, for a set fee.

The day of the shoot arrives and Bart arrives on the scene, with cameras and film. To make his life a bit easier, he has a bellhop carry his cameras to his first shooting location while he takes care of some details. Subsequently, our enterprising friend takes his shots and everything goes off without a hitch—until he gets the film back from the lab.

All of the film Bart shot is unusable. There are light streaks and other strange phenomena over all his slides. Now, he has to go back to the client and tell him what happened. Not only does the *business* lose some of their reputation, but Bart had committed a large part of the business's ready cash to buy film and rent specialized equipment—which he would have been reimbursed for later by the client if the shoot had worked out. And why didn't the shoot work out?

When the bellhop carried the equipment, he dropped the cameras, unbeknownst to Bart. This created a light leak, making all of the film shot on this assignment unusable. So, when Adam returned from his trip a few days later, he found that the business was not only running in the red, there was nothing he could do about it except ball out his partner and go out and hustle up some new business.

Of course, the law will not allow a partner to get away with just anything. For instance, one partner cannot give away the cameras, film, and other equipment that belongs to the business without his partner's approval. For that matter a partner cannot do anything that would subsequently make it untenable for the business to continue. Realize, however, that while the law *says* a partner cannot do anything of the sort, he can still do it. Then it becomes necessary for one partner to take legal action against the other to force him to make restitution. Not that it does a whole lot of good. While the case is being decided in court, no work can be done without equipment!

For a photographer first going into business who doesn't have enough ready capital to make a go of it, a limited partnership can be an ideal arrangement.

First, you seek out an investor. It can be a relative, a friend, or even an entrepeneur who just wants to make an investment.

Second, the photographer takes the invested money and sets up the business. With such an arrangement, the partner investing the money agrees to leave the day-to-day operation of the business to the photographer. The photographer is then left to operate the business as if he was the sole proprietor. His partner has a specific profit participation that has been agreed upon. So, if the photographer's business prospers, the partner putting up the money may not only recoup his investment, but make a profit also. In contrast, if the photographer's business fails, his partner loses his investment.

Usually, the partner putting up the money is not liable for any more revenue unless this is agreed upon initially or a rider to the original agreement is inserted at a later date. So, for instance, if in the first few months of being in business, the photographer is operating at a loss (his expenses are more than his net profit), he may ask his partner for more money to keep the business afloat. If no agreement exists, then the photographer may, at that point, have to find another line of work.

Now, supposing the partner supplying the capital sees that the business is in the red, and it looks like it will be for some time to come. Regardless of his initial investment, he's still liable for his percentage of the business's indebtedness. He may choose to cut his losses at this point by serving the photographer with a written notice that he is no longer a partner and is exiting the business. Then, he is only liable for his percentage of the debts incurred up to this time. The photographer is left to make good the debts incurred after receiving the written notice, and at any time in the future, if he elects to stay in business as a sole proprietor.

*Ending a Partnership.* As you can see, being in a partnership has its hazards. The worst aspect of a partnership is the very real possibility that the friend/partner might not be such a friend when times get tough. So, to protect yourself, make sure that you insert into your partnership agreement, which a lawyer has drawn up, a provision for termination of the partnership agreement.

Specify in the partnership agreement under what conditions either party may terminate the agreement. For instance, you might want a provision saying that if one partner goes personally bankrupt, the partnership agreement is terminated. Why add this provision? To prevent your partner's creditors from attempting to attach the assets of your joint business to pay for *his* debts. Now, the creditors may not have a legal leg to stand on: Still, they can make the effort, and at the least, get a legal hold on the business's available capital. Believe me, you don't need this aggravation.

Try to think about business and personal relationships in the abstract when putting together the termination provision, as well as the partnership agreement as a whole. Remember Murphy's Law: "Everything that can go wrong, will go wrong."

## INCORPORATING

A corporation is a legal entity composed of a number of individuals who do business as if they were one individual. When incorporating, the individuals who are doing business as one pay the state for a charter and a corporate seal.

On a practical level, a photographer may incorporate by making his relatives and/or friends the officers of the corporation—officers being required by law. The photographer still makes all the decisions and functions as a sole proprietor.

What's the advantage to incorporating, given the fact that it costs money to buy the charter and the corporate seal necessary?

The liability of a corporation is limited. In general, the members do not have any personal liability toward the corporation's unsecured (a member hasn't signed for the debts personally) debts beyond the amount of individual shares they hold in the corporation. So, if your incorporated photography business goes bankrupt, you, the photographer, can only be held liable for your investment in the corporation, nothing more. Assuming the debts are unsecured, your personal finances cannot be attached to cover the corporation's liability.

There are disadvantages to incorporating also. Incorporating takes money. To do it, as much as five hundred dollars is needed in some states. When you're first starting out in business, five hundred dollars is a lot of money.

If you've incorporated under Internal Revenue Service Subchapter S, and your corporation (photography business) makes a profit, those monies can then be taxed as if they were part of your own personal income tax return. Correspondingly, S corporation stockholders can write off corporate losses as if they were personal losses, on their income tax returns.

## WHICH LEGAL ENTITY DO I CHOOSE?

Individual Ownership. General or Limited Partnership. Corporation. Which one do you choose?

If you have few assets, go for the individual ownership. You won't have the further hassles of dealing with a partner or corporate tax law intricacies.

If you have large personal assets and investments, incorporate. Your personal as well as business income might benefit.

If you're someplace in-between financially, then consider a partnership. The added capital from a partner can make the difference between a flourishing or a floundering business. Any aggravation involved with having to cope with a partner will pale as a business grows and stays successful.

## OTHER CONSIDERATIONS

Once you have made the decision regarding the form that the business will take, there are seemingly minor details to deal with. Since these details, however, will be a part of your impact upon your potential clients, they are just as important.

*The business name.* Every business has to have a name. Most photographers who deal with clients other than wedding and portrait photographers, usually opt for their own name, followed by the word photographer. A business card could read as simply as: PETER PARKER, PHOTOGRAPHER.

If you are going to be relying directly on the public for your business, consider creating a name for your business other than your given and surnames. PETER PARKER, PHOTOGRAPHER might be changed to read, PARKSON PHOTOGRAPHY. The latter sounds more business-like.

*Post office box or home address.* If you are going to have a business address (studio), where all your business correspondence is forwarded, you won't need a post office box number.

A post office box number is usually used by photographers who want to disguise the fact that they are doing business from their home, which many clients consider to be unbusiness-like. Sometimes they are going to use a number of different locations, like space that is sublet, to do their business, and therefore will not have one, permanent business address.

If you are going to use your home address for business correspondence, make sure that on your stationary, envelopes and business cards, you identify yourself either by your business name, or by your name, followed by the word "photographer." This keeps all of your correspondence on a business level.

*Stationary and business cards.* Stationary and business cards should contain the name of your business (if any), your name, address, and phone number, including area code. Keep the design simple and don't use any fancy crests that printers sometimes suggest. They look ridiculous.

Make sure that the envelopes have your name and return address printed on them. Typing this information in, or using a cheap, rubber stamp version looks horrible.

*Business or personal phone listing.* If you plan on doing most of your business with the public, it pays to go to the extra cost of getting a business phone listing with the phone company. This way, your business gets listed in the Yellow Pages, for easy reference by potential customers.

A business phone listing is generally a good idea for any photographer with a studio space. Even fashion and commercial photographers, who deal with individual clients rather than the public, will want to project as businesslike an impression as possible. A separate business phone listing helps.

If you plan on being a freelancer, that is, not working in any one category in particular, you don't have to go to the additional cost of getting a separate business phone. A personal listing will suffice.

*Long distance telephone services.* Chances are there will be quite a few instances where it will be necessary to make long distance telephone calls. I recommend using one of the long distance services available—separate from AT&T. They tend to be less expensive. Sprint, MCI, and SBS Skyline are good choices, but check their rates and services before you buy.

*Answering service or answering machine.* Some photographers will tell you that they prefer the personal touch, so they elect to purchase the services of a phone answering service. Others say that the additional cost of paying for a phone answering service every month, rather than the one-time cost for a telephone answering machine, is unwarranted.

Who's right? It does sound more professional when a person answers your phone rather than a machine. I don't feel, however, that the additional cost of the service, at least at the beginning of your photography business, is necessary.

I suggest getting a good, reliable phone answering machine with a beeper. The beeper will allow you to go anywhere in the world, but still be in contact with your business. You simply dial your phone number and "beep" your phone with the beeper. The tone from the beeper will automatically rewind your answering machine, which will play back the message you received while in the field.

I've had a couple of answering machines and the best I've had is a Sanyo TAS 3000. It was relatively inexpensive to purchase, at the time of this writing had the smallest beeper available, and it's been very reliable. It can also function as a dictation device.

## CHAPTER SIX

# KEEPING ACCURATE RECORDS

The photographer has other business considerations. He has to keep a set of books so he knows what his debits and credits are. The photographer has to know which business expenses are tax deductible and which aren't. In short, he's going to need the advice of an accountant.

It is constantly amazing to me how many photographers I've run into who insist upon doing their own books, their own income tax returns, and never even bother consulting with an accountant.

These photographers think they are saving the accountant's fee. After all, why pay an accountant for something they can do themselves? If their clients thought like this, they'd probably wind up never getting a job because the client's would say, "Gee, I can shoot this job. Why should I give it to a photographer?" The answer is the photographer can do a better and more professional job, and the same thing holds true with an accountant.

A good accountant is as vital to your business as a good camera. He knows the tax laws. You don't. I can also tell you from personal experience that a good accountant can keep a business going when times are tough.

When I first started out in business for myself, I had no idea about what to do as far as my books were concerned. I knew next to nothing about keeping records of expenses, everything from typewriter ribbon to film processing receipts. I knew nothing about schedule C and schedule E. All I knew was that, as a person on staff at a photography magazine, I got a W-2 form at the end of the year, had my accountant fill out my income tax returns, and if I was lucky, I didn't owe the government anything.

As a self-employed individual, I found out that much of my income could be written off as a business expense, which meant I didn't have to pay tax on it. So I was free to pump that money saved back into the business and help it grow. The person who taught me what it means to be an "independent" is Lee Fox. Fox is an accountant with 12 years of experience, who works for *Lawrence Kaufman and Company*, a public accounting firm based in mid-town Manhattan. Fox's clients include professional photographers and business people in a number of different areas.

When I contacted him for this book, he was able to give me some time to sit down and specifically discuss the business of photography. Because he had so many informative and interesting things to say, I'm presenting our interview on the following pages in the question and answer format.

We met over coffee in Fox's office on a hot summer's day. The air-conditioning was going full blast, and like any good accountant, Fox was dressed in the uniform of his trade: pin-striped, three-piece suit, shirt, and tie.

## AN ACCOUNTANT'S VIEW

*Can you give us a specific way for a photographer to set up his books?*

Sure. The photographer is in a service business. He's not required to use the accrual basis of accounting, meaning he doesn't have to realize income when he bills out. So, the simplest way of keeping your books is to record your income when you receive it and record your expenses when you pay them. When you're working a non-inventory business like photography, you also have the *choice* of using either cash or an accrual basis.

*Which means what?*

You have the choice of how you're going to account for your income—when you collect it or when you earn it. Accrual is when you earn it, cash is when you collect it. A typical example: on December 15 you bill $50,000 worth of work. You don't collect it until January. On the cash basis of accounting, you wouldn't report that income until next year's income tax return. Under the accrual basis, you report the income when you bill it (December 15), which means it would go on this year's income tax return. If there are no expenses against it, you're going to end up paying taxes before you collect the money in the latter case.

*Then why account for your income on the accrual basis?*

Well, you have the choice. In a non-service business, you don't have that choice. Accounting principles dictate that the income cycle is finished when you've done whatever it takes to do to earn the income. Whether you collect it or not is your problem. That's what the definition of accounts receivable is. The earning process is complete so you've earned the income. Most photographers would therefore use the cash basis.

Now, to set up your books, what you basically need is a cash receipts journal and a cash disbursements journal. The cash receipts journal is just a list of the monies you've received that are going into the bank that you realized on a specific job. In 95% of the cases, it's going to be income. A cash disbursements journal is really a classification and abstract of your checkbook showing what you're spending the money on and what it's for. The excess of the income over the expenses is your profit. This is the easiest way to set up your books. And, if you keep a set of books like this, they are invaluable should you get audited by the Internal Revenue Service.

*How would you go about choosing an accountant?*

Well, generally, you don't walk in off the street and say to someone, "Would you like to be my accountant?"

*You're not going to recommend H&R Block, are you?*

H&R Block is generally a tax preparation service, and you can go to them if you have the expertise of keeping your own books. But H&R Block is not usually involved in ongoing business activity. Generally, you choose an accountant by recommendation from other people that you know in business. Another way to pick an accountant is to consult with the CPA societies that we have in many of the states. These societies have a list of accounting firms that specialize in certain areas. So, one could call his CPA state society and ask them if they have a list of any accountants that specialize in photography.

*What about fees? If a photographer has an accountant working for him, would he come in occasionally, take a look at the books and make sure things are correct?*

Yes. That's what an accountant will do, but it's very hard to give a range of fees. You're dealing with different levels of accounting. A fellow who works out of his house and doesn't have much overhead may not charge much for his services. If you went to a national accounting firm, which has a department specializing in small businesses, they could charge you as much as $200 an hour.

*So for a guy who doesn't have a lot of cash, like the beginning photographer, he's probably better off going with a small firm that's reputable?*

You're right. Because in a small firm you get more personalized service. The only other problem is, that even with a small firm, it depends who you get. If you're a small client, most of the work will be done by a "junior." Some juniors are knowledgeable, some aren't. But many times, in order to save some money, you let the "junior" do the actual work, and use the partner or the manager as a consultant. See, the photographer will save money that way, because a principal in a small firm, his time can go for $125 an hour. The "junior" only bills out at $40 an hour.

*Is there any way the photographer can keep up with the IRS regulations himself, or are they too complicated?*

It'd be rather hard, considering he has a business to run. That's why there are accountants.

*In the case of an audit, would the accountant accompany the photographer, in return for charging a certain fee for that service?*

Oh, definitely. Usually, all these things are discussed up front, when you're hiring the accountant. The photographer should find out what the accountant is going to be charging, what his engagement will consist of, and what services he will provide. Accountants generally put the terms of their contract with a photographer into what is called an engagement letter.

*Turning to a different topic, let's talk about expansion. Supposing the photographer has been in business for awhile, he's getting more and more work coming in and he now wants to expand. How would an accountant fit into that scenario?*

Generally when you expand, you need money. The accountant is called upon to prepare projections and cash flow statements because when you're going to a bank or another institution to finance it, they want to know exactly what you expect to do with the money, and how you're going to repay the loan. Also, the accountant is used to provide an internal projection: if you're going to make a specific level of income, is it worth your while to expand? Is there enough in it for the principal to want to expand? Many times you can double your business, get the headaches of doubling your business, and not get enough of a return for it. Many times it's not worth a photographer's while to get too big.

*You mean with expansion, added expenses eat up profits?*

It can happen. The main thing people want to know is, 'what's in it for me?' So, the accountant would extrapolate the expansion figures, and you'd see if it was worth your while after the additional expenses involved with expanding. You could have a $50,000 business, make $20,000 in profit, but find that if you go to $100,000, the expenses would be so great, that your profit was only $25,000.

*Aside from getting business loans, is there another way to finance your business, specifically getting equipment?*

Many times when you want to buy your equipment, you'll find out that there are finance companies who will lease it to you. They may require a personal guarantee that you're liable if you go under, but they are usually involved, those finance companies, with the people selling the equipment, who really want to make the sale. You'll have to pay interest, though, on the loan.

*When you're first going into business, let's say with a storefront studio or even a loft. How much money will you need?*

In general, you'll have to have at least three months expenses up front. This would cover rent, payroll, payments on your equipment, everything. And what about building a portfolio? That's another expense, though it is an investment.

*What is tax deductible in a photographer's business?*

Generally, anything or any monies that are spent in order to keep the business running. This will include monies spent on film. Equipment is amortized over a period of time. Also, cab fares to see a client about a job, the monies spent taking clients out to lunch where you discuss business, the rent on your studio, interest on your loans, props and costumes that are necessary for a shoot and that you don't have a budget from the client for, answering machines and services, stationary and business cards, costs of hiring models when you don't have a budget for that from a client (like you're doing a test), promotional materials, the percentage of your income that you pay your rep, any income paid to photographer's assistants and office help, the accountant's fee. In short everything that is necessary, as I said, to make the business work. Your accountant will tell you exactly what is and isn't deductible.

*How about keeping a separate diary of business appointments?*

That's a good idea too. This establishes a business sequence, states on which days you had appointments and allied expenses, like cab fares and lunches, as well as who you met. Should you be audited, it's nice to have a diary to bring along to prove you do what you say you do.

## THE INTERNAL REVENUE SERVICE AUDIT

Now suppose you do everything Lee Fox suggests. You hire an accountant, you keep your books and still, something spits out of the I.R.S. computer, and one day, that dreaded brown envelope is in your mailbox. You open it and lo and behold, you're being summoned to a royal audience with your local I.R.S. man.

The first reaction is to panic. I know. I've been audited and I can tell you from experience that it isn't all that bad. In my case, the I.R.S. had questioned, ironically, my medical expenses. The computer had spit out that in my tax bracket, my medical expenses were too high. I was "asked" to appear for a hearing 30 days from the time I received my letter.

Immediately, I called Fox. He explained to me that I could get an extension before I had to show up. This would give me time to go over my books and get everything together.

I decided, after Fox briefed me, to go down to the I.R.S. myself because I didn't want to pay Fox's day rate. In retrospect, this was a foolish move, even though things did work out. But I didn't know that at the time.

Armed with my diary and another notebook of cash receipts and cash disbursements, as well as receipts for all expenses for the tax year in question, I showed up at my local I.R.S. office. I had a cold and was totally miserable. I had visions of being stuck in jail for non-payment of taxes and having my mother visit me with chicken soup. (Considering my mother lives in Florida, it would have been a long commute up to New York and my cold, gray jail cell.)

When at last I was called by my I.R.S. examiner, I was ushered through a maze of cubicles, until I reached my examiner's humble plastic chair, plastic divider, and probably plastic desk.

During the first part of the examination, I realized that the examiner was as nervous as I was, which made me relax a bit. Quickly, we went over the medical expenses, all of which he said he would "allow." This meant I didn't have to pay additional taxes on those expenses.

Going over my business expenses, my receipts and diary of appointments proved I did what I did. He found no discrepancies, but then, at the last minute, he realized there was a place on the return where *I* had forgotten to record a business expense. I wound up having to pay an additional $200 in taxes, which was okay with me and my mother, who saved on plane fare.

My experience with the I.R.S. proved that they were simply out to do their job in the best way possible, that they weren't out for my scalp, and they really were rather polite. So, don't worry if you wind up being audited. It happens to many people in business for themselves.

## INSURANCE OPTIONS

One other aspect of running your photography business is getting insurance. There are a number of different types of insurance that you'll need. I spoke with Adrienne Isquith, a special agent with the Northwest Mutual Life Insurance Company, in her office in Queens, New York.

"The first thing you're going to need is liability. This is insurance that covers injury for *anyone* on the premises of your studio." If you're going to be using large props and scenary that could fall, animals that can maim and injure, or any sort of heavy equipment, liability insurance is an absolute *must.*

"You should also carry," Isquith continues, "multi-peril insurance. This will cover you for fire and theft in the studio, as well as theft of equipment on location.

"Next, in many states like New York, you need disability and worker's compensation insurance for full-time employees. It's the law. Disability covers an employee if they have a non-work related illness or accident, while worker's compensation covers an employee who hurts himself on the premises. For example, if a photographer's assistant who's a full-time employee gets hit by a car on his way home from work, the disability facet of your insurance package will pay his salary. If a view camera falls on his foot and breaks his toe during a shoot, requiring recuperation at home, the worker's compensation part of the package will pay his salary.

"The photographer who's self-employed can also take out disability insurance on himself, which would cover him should he be hurt on or off the job."

How about other medical insurance for the photographer and his full-time employees?

"The photographer should have some sort of health insurance," Isquith answers. "Health insurance that's provided under a basic plan, like the one Blue Cross/Blue Shield sells, covers hospitalization, the costs of in-hospital services and other health related expenses which your individual policy can outline. You should also get a good major medical policy which covers additional hospitalization expenses that the basic health insurance plan doesn't cover." I should also add that if the photographer is 65 years or older, Medicare payments from the United States government will also help defray medical expenses.

"If you can," Isquith explains, "you may also want to implement a pension plan for yourself. This would include a pension plan for full-time employees and for the self-employed photographer. I'd recommend a Keogh-type plan. You may also implement a medical plan for your employees, but both the pension and medical plans for employees are optional.

"Also, make sure you have the automobile insurance for your car or van, and make sure to tell the insurance agent whether the means of transportation is used for business and/or personal pleasure.

"One other thing I would add is life insurance. Especially if a photographer has a family to support, life insurance is a good thing to have."

Adrienne Isquith also pointed out to me that it would be impossible to give you exact figures on the cost of insurance in general. The cost is determined by a number of different criteria that would be different for every photographer, including age, health status, the location of the studio, and the amount of insurance coverage you wish to carry in each category I've just outlined.

## CHAPTER SEVEN

# SELECTING THE EQUIPMENT

---

Your business has been legally formed. You have the capital to open the doors to your studio, and you have the confidence that you'll succeed. Now you need to select the equipment for your business.

You're going to need professional quality equipment. Equipment that is rugged, reliable, and can stand up to a variety of foul weather conditions is a must.

### EVALUATING ENDORSEMENTS

If you read photography magazines at all, you've probably seen ads where one famous photographer or another extolls the virtues of a particular camera or certain lenses. In my experience, most of the time the photographer is being paid for the use of his name. He may not even be a user of the product he's endorsing. An ad agency copywriter writes the words that appear under the photographer's byline in the ad.

So, don't let those ads sway your decision about which cameras, lenses, or equipment to purchase.

### FORMATS

When selecting cameras and lenses, you'll need to decide which of the three different photographic formats you'll be using. Cameras and lenses that record images on 35mm film are considered small format equipment. The measurement diagonally across the negative, from one corner to the other, is 35mm.

Medium format, sometimes referred to as 2¼″ equipment, records images on 120 and 220 roll film. These cameras produce negatives that are larger than their 35mm counterpart. The image size depends on the camera model. For instance, Hasselblad cameras produce a negative that is 6 × 6 cm or 2¼″-square. Other manufacturers produce cameras that have negative size of 6 × 4.5 cm (2¼″ × 1⅝″) or 6 × 7 cm (2¼″ × 2¾″).

At the other end of the spectrum are the view or large format cameras and lenses. The negative from this type of camera can also vary. It may be 4″ × 5″ or 8″ × 10″.

In general, the larger the format, the more expensive the equipment. For instance, you can get a very good 35mm SLR for $300, but a comparable medium format Hasselblad or large format Sinar Bron camera runs into the thousands of dollars.

*Why one format rather than the other?* The answer to this question is two-fold. Certain types of jobs, like portraits, food photography, certain types of product photography, and landscape photography, require the clarity and perspective control that you can only get when you use a view camera. Both 4 × 5 and 8 × 10 negatives make cropping easy because they are so large. Printing from the larger negative is also excellent because you don't have to worry about the grain that usually results when you enlarge a smaller negative.

Other jobs, like advertising, bookcover, and wedding photography may look especially good in the squarer, medium format. In addition, the medium format negative, while not as large as the one the view camera yields, is never-the-less sharper and clearer than a 35mm negative.

The 35mm camera is preferred by photojournalists, fashion, aerial, and annual report photographers because of its light weight and versatility. It's easier to change lenses, attach filters, and so forth. Photographers also use 35mm photography for a variety of commercial jobs.

The client may also require a particular format. It is not uncommon for an art director, magazine editor, or any other client to tell you what format he wants you to use. That's why a photographer has to be able to work in the three formats with equal dexterity. Without this ability, you may lose a job. For instance, what would you do if a client asked you to shoot a job with a view camera, when you've never even looked through one?

*How much equipment should I buy?* "Get two of everything," advises Alan Zenreich. Zenreich is a successful Manhattan photographer, specializing in still lifes/special effects work. "And make sure that's two of everything, in every format," he adds.

Zenreich's advice is well-taken, but it is difficult to provide the capital in one lump sum to get "two of everything." Zenreich is quick to point out that all of his equipment, in the three formats, was accumulated over many years as a professional photographer. That's tens of thousands of dollars worth of cameras, lenses, and lights. You should also bear in mind that you can always rent equipment for a particular job.

## 35MM EQUIPMENT

Since 35mm equipment is the most inexpensive, and among professional photographers, the most common staple in their photographic arsenal, let's deal with 35mm photography first.

Almost any job can be shot on 35mm. That's not to say that you couldn't do a better job on some assignments with medium and large format equipment; you could. But a 35mm system of photography from a major camera manufacturer is something you have to have.

Dave Metz, a national technical representative for Canon, U.S.A., Inc., who frequently counsels professional photographers on their equipment needs, has some advice for the photographer who plans on being a generalist—a category most of you will fall into at least at the beginning of your career. While his recommendations obviously encompass only Canon products, you can digest his information generically and substitute your equipment favorites for Canon equipment, should you so desire.

"I'd recommend that the beginning photographer get 2 F1 bodies, with motor drive or winders for each. Then, a 100mm macro lens and macro light, which would be useful for a science or other medically oriented assignment," Dave begins. He continues:

"I'd also get a 20mm lens that's good for outdoor and indoor architectural shots, a 24mm *f*/1.4 for group shots, a 50mm *f*/1.2 for existing light situations, an 85mm *f*/1.2 for portrait work, an 85mm soft focus lens for special effects work, a 135mm *f*/2 for sports and photojournalistic shots, and a 200mm *f*/2.8 and 300mm *f*/2.8. These two lenses are excellent for sports work or anything else for that matter, when you're going to be a long distance away from your subject.

"If you're going to be concentrating on architectural work, get a 35mm tilt and shift lens for altering perspective. For weddings, I suggest using a versatile zoom, like the Canon 35mm to 105mm zoom. Also, get a variety of focusing screens so focusing is made easy, a good studio flash system—like the one Balcar makes—a dedicated top-mounting flash system, like the Canon 533G, and a speed finder for sports and close-up work. For extra close, close-ups, you can also attach a 6X (six times) magnifier."

Dave Metz's suggestions when enacted upon, would give you an ideal equipment set-up.

## 35MM EQUIPMENT INFORMATION

In this particular format, I do have a personal recommendation. I have always used Nikons and Nikon lenses and never found them wanting. In fact, I recently shot the Mendenhall Glacier in Alaska and the temperature on the glacier was about 37 degrees farenheit. My Nikon FE, my personal favorite, kept working, the battery and film transport mechanism never failed and the pictures turned out great.

I have also found that most of the photographers I come in contact with use Nikons. They feel that Nikon equipment has a well-deserved reputation for consistently high quality of product. It is rugged and dependable. Next to Nikon, I've found some professionals who prefer Canon, with Olympus and Minolta as the next two choices.

Listing all the models available from each of these manufacturers would be difficult at best. The market is ever-changing, but I did ask the manufacturers for some specific recommendations for professional photographers.

Nikon recommends the FE2. This model has a shutter speed range of 8 seconds to 1/4000 second—quite handy to have in certain types of situations. It also has a flash synchronization speed of 1/250 second which is also very useful. This model has improved vibration controls that make slow hand-held shots (at 1/60 or 1/30) yield much more acceptable results. As with most models, the camera accepts a multitude of accessories and also has a very sensitive metering system which can give accurate results in very low-light situations.

Canon recommends the F1. The F1 has a removeable prism (with interchangeable focusing screens) which allows you to change the metering system from center-weighted to selective area to spot metering. The shutter can be operated mechanically from 1/250 to 1/2000—a definite asset if the battery goes dead.

Olympus recommends the OM-2S Program. This model has a

metering system that sets both the shutter speed and the aperture. The camera can also be operated as an aperture-preferred model or a manual model. The exposure system has two mirrors which allows for changes (exposure adjustments) even while the shutter is operating.

Minolta recommends the X-570. The X-570 has an automatic exposure lock that allows you to approach your subject, meter it, lock in the reading, and then compose the entire shot. This is a feature that will enable the photographer to adjust for extreme lighting situations. This model also has an automatic flash exposure control. With the appropriate dedicated flash unit, the camera will adjust the flash emission for proper exposure.

*Independent Lens Manufacturers.* There are a number of other companies that are not affiliated with the major camera and lens manufacturers. These companies e.g., Soligor and Vivitar, make their own brand of lenses that fit just about any 35mm SLR on the market.

Again, among professional photographers I've spoken with, the quality of the Vivitar optics is always mentioned and preferred.

I have tried one of the Vivitar zooms, the 75mm to 205mm Macro Focusing Zoom, and was impressed with the clarity of the finished photograph and the ease with which I could switch back-and-forth to my other Nikkor lenses.

Try some of these other independent lens manufacturers' products before you make your final selection. Again, you can write manufacturers for information so you can compare the various features. (see Appendix)

*Choosing the System.* In reality, you are choosing more than a camera—you are choosing a system that will no doubt include various lenses and other accessories. Because of the variations in the type of equipment available, you must weigh your choices carefully.

One way to compare systems before you even compare prices is to write to the various manufacturers for product information on the model/models you are considering (see Appendix). You can also check the consumer publications and photography magazines that rate equipment.

After you have narrowed down your selection somewhat, comparison shop. Generally the cameras will be priced lower than the manufacturer's suggested price. You should also try out the various models to see how they feel to you. The size, weight, and convenience of controls may seem irrelevant at the time of purchase, but they will matter in the ease of handling during an actual shoot.

## MEDIUM FORMAT

Companies that make medium-format equipment include Rollei, Bronica, Pentax and Mamiya. But without a doubt, the champion in this format category is Hasselblad.

The name Hasselblad is synonymous with quality. I know it sounds like I'm doing public relations for the company, but it's true. I have never yet heard a professional photographer say a bad word about Hasselblad cameras and lenses, and the overwhelming majority of professional photographers that I know use Hasselblads.

Ernst Wildi, the Technical Director of Victor Hasselblad, Inc., has some specific suggestions for your equipment requirements. Once again, you may substitute any other equipment favorites in the medium-format category, for Hasselblad equipment.

"For the wedding and portrait photographer, I have the following suggestions," Wildi begins.

"A Hasselblad 500 C/M body, with the 60mm CF Distagon lens and the 150mm CF Sonnar lens. Also, get at least 2 magazines, either 2 of the A12s or 2 A24s. Include in your package 1 professional lens shade, 1 Softar #2, (a lens accessory) and 1 flashgun bracket, with the flash itself made by another company."

For the commercial or industrial photographer, Wildi has these suggestions:

"A Hasselblad 2000FCW body with an 80mm CF Planar. Other lenses you'll need are the 50mm CF Distagon and the 120mm CF Macro Planar. Then, remember to get the professional lens shade and at least 2 film magazines A12 and 1 Polaroid film magazine."

## MEDIUM FORMAT INFORMATION

Again listing all the makes and models available for each of the manufacturers is somewhat pointless. Given the changing market, the list would be dated before the book is reprinted!

Before actual models can be discussed, however, there are some differences in this format that are crucial. The cameras are often available with different backs. These backs will allow for the use of 120 or 220 roll film. In some instances, the backs will also allow for a change in negative size.

The other major deciding factor is the type of shutter available. A focal plane shutter is in the camera body. A leaf shutter is housed in the lens. Now, some specifics.

Zenza Bronica's latest entry is the multi-format GS-1. This model has a leaf shutter, interchangeable backs for various size negatives—in this instance from the standard 35mm to 6 × 7cm! This model has off-the-film metering capabilities with a flash, provided you have the speed grip which houses the necessary electronics.

Mamiya's RZ67 ProS is also a leaf shutter model. It is a 6 × 7cm format that can accept 120 or 220 film backs. The revolving back on this model allows you to frame either horizontally or vertically (without becoming a contortionist in the process).

Pentax 645 is a 6 × 4.5 cm camera with aperture-preferred, shutter-preferred, and program auto modes with through-the-lens metering for flash, *and* a built-in motor wind! It has a focal plane shutter and a non-interchangeable prism. It will accept film holders for 120, 220, and 70mm film.

Rollei's model 6006 contains a built-in motor and is capable of shutter-preferred exposure. It will accept backs for 120 and 220 film. The interchangeable backs allow for negatives in the 6 × 6 cm or 6 × 4.5 cm format. Another important note in this model is the newly designed dark slide—this slide rolls out of the way. It will "disappear" inside the holder.

*Choosing the System.* Basically, you can follow the same procedure that you would for choosing a 35mm system. There are some decisions you will have to make that are slightly different because of the many options in this format. The size of the negative you will want to have will undoubtly influence your choice. For example, many of the less expensive models will not provide you with the options that a GS-1 can. Remember, too, that interchangeable backs can be rather expensive, and you should always have a spare—*in the same format.* The backs will also determine whether or not you use 120 or 220 roll film. Both of these choices will determine how many photographs you will get on one roll of film—another important consideration depending on the type of work you will use this system for.

Most models are sold with a waist-level finder. This type of finder projects the image upside-down. The use of a prism finder will rectify this, but it is another expense you'll have to consider. While I'm on the subject of prisms, in most cases, the meter is also housed in the prism—not the camera. If you are considering the prism as an alternative to viewing everything upside-down, you might also consider whether or not to invest in a prism that has a metering system included. If you choose to buy a "plain" prism, you will have to use another type of exposure meter.

Although it sounds complicated and expensive to invest in this type of format, it does have advantages. Even with a 2¼″-square model, you'll have a negative that is 3½ times the size of a 35mm negative. The size will help limit the grain problems when making enlargements. Image quality (technically, of course) will improve. The cropping possibilities will increase and retouching (if necessary) will be easier.

Again, study your particular needs. Handle the models you are interested in because the difference between 35mm and medium format is considerable, but you can adapt to it.

## LARGE FORMAT INFORMATION

The best way to illustrate the benefits of using large format equipment is to quote someone who earns his living using it.

"I've been in business 23 years," says Boston-based photographer Steve Grohe. "It was an assignment 20 years ago that made me switch from 35mm to large format.

"We did some work for a publishing firm and they ordered 30 × 30 black-and-white prints. My assistant and I worked all night with those incredibly small negatives to get the job done. Afterwards, I said to myself, 'You're crazy. When are you going to go into view cameras and stop fooling around with these small negatives?' "

Grohe made the switch. And what are some of the other reasons he prefers working in large format?

Grohe likes the higher quality and better resolution of the view camera transparency. It's also become a necessity for him to shoot in large format. Much of the computer hardware he shoots during assignments covering annual reports, brochures, ads, and trade magazine covers, has a lifespan of only two to three years before it becomes obsolete. So, if Grohe were to do the job in 35mm there could be as much as a two week delay for sandwiching and other special optical work. That two weeks represents a significant amount of time in the life of the product he's shooting.

"What I like to do on the special effects shots, where we're trying to make the computers look really high-tech, is to sandwich my exposures," Grohe explains. "I'll build an image on one sheet of film by taking a number of exposures.

"For a zoom technique that I like to use, I'll advance the lens on the camera column toward the subject. There are three, discrete movements that I use to move the lens in calculated increments. On the final shot, you can see how the colors advance and recede from the eye. I call it romanticizing technology."

Grohe says that he's become particularly fond of shooting with wide-angle lenses.

"There was one job where we were shooting a cable, which was the client's product. We placed it on the set we'd built in the studio, so the cable was stretching directly in front of the camera. By using a 65mm wide-angle lens, the photo certainly looked normal. But the cable stretched in front of the camera looked huge. That size denoted the power of the product, which was what the client wanted in the shot. I'd say that was a successful shoot."

Another interesting view camera assignment involved the Civil War.

"There was another shoot I did for the cover of a computer trade magazine. We created models of the Monitor and the Merrimac, the Union and Confederate iron-clads that fought it out during the Civil War. On one of the models, we stripped in a computer, so it looked like the computer was on the front of, and acting as the brains, for the ship. And again, because we were working in large format, there was no problem for the magazine's art director as to where to place the cover's typeface. I left plenty of room at the top of the shot."

Would Grohe ever consider going back to shooting with a 35mm?

"Never," he says emphatically. "I don't even own a 35mm SLR. The smallest camera I have is a Hasselblad!"

## LARGE FORMAT EQUIPMENT INFORMATION

Some of the companies that produce large format equipment include Sinar Bron and Berkey Omega. Here's a description of the view camera equipment they've recommended for the professional photographer.

Sinar is recommending their Sinar P camera. It's fully compatible with the Sinar system of view camera photography established over 35 years ago.

The patented asymmetric tilt system of the Sinar P locates the horizontal and vertical tilt axes exactly in the film plane. With the Sinar P, you can control sharpness distribution or adjust perspective without refocusing. This system makes precise sharpness control fully straightforward. On the Sinar P, even the image format can be matched to any assignment without complex conversion.

Three alternative rear standards are available for the Sinar P to take the nominal $4 \times 5$, $5 \times 7$ and $8 \times 10$ formats. The rear standards take all sheet films of any size, roll films in appropriate magazines and most instant picture materials, in sheet film or film pack form, up to $8'' \times 10''$.

The $4'' \times 5''$ back has an additional housing for a meter probe of in-film plane light meter systems. With a simple swivel motion, you bring the meter probe into the viewing screen area and take spot readings of flash or continuous light directly on the film plane, without the need of a separate light meter cassette.

All of this comes in a solid universal case, when you buy the expert Sinar P outfit.

Berkey Omega is recommending their Omega View/Toyo 45D for the professional entering the large format field. Its key features include a 360 degree revolving back with bail arm for maximum composing freedom and ease of use. It also has easy-to-apply reference scales for tilts, lateral shifts, and rise movements. It accepts all standard $4 \times 5$ sheet film holders, Polaroid Land Film Holder Model 545, film packs, and Graflok accessories. A large monorail is used for maximum rigidity with an elevated monorail rib that maintains precise alignment of front and rear standards. The dual function spirit level on the rear standard aids in precision alignment.

The 45D works with a wide range of accessories, both unique to the 45D and/or compatible with the entire Omega View/Toya large format system.

*Choosing the System.* In this instance, you must remember that the large format system is the most expensive system that you can buy. You will have to weigh the possible returns on your investment very carefully.

Because of the amount of money involved, I recommend that you try out each system at your local camera store. After you have decided on the model that you prefer, contact the manufacturer and request a demonstration of the equipment *before* you make the actual purchase.

## OTHER EQUIPMENT

Once you have purchased your camera or cameras, you will have to consider the additional equipment that you'll need. This will depend on the type of work that you do or, in some cases, the specific requirements of a particular job.

*Film.* Kodak, Fuji, Agfa, Ilford, and 3M make a variety of color and black-and-white emulsions. Try a number of emulsions by different companies to see which ones work best for you. When you find emulsions that consistently meet your picture-taking requirements, stay with them, until something better comes along.

*Tripods.* You're going to need the steady support of a tripod during shooting, so you wind up with perfectly registered images.

The tripod lines manufactured by Slik, Bogen, Tilt All, and Gitzo are rugged and dependable. Each of these companies makes a number of different types of tripods, from friction to fluid heads.

*Studio Lighting Systems.* On some studio jobs where you're not using available light, you're going to need a studio lighting system to provide the additional illumination.

Studio lighting systems are more versatile than their on-camera counterpart, the electronic strobe. Since the studio unit is not directly connected to the camera, there are few, if any, limitations to the positions you can use when shooting products, or models.

Speedotron and Balcar make power packs, strobe heads, and light stands that are versatile enough to fill the requirements of any photographic assignment. You can buy power packs, strobe heads, and light stands separately, or in a package deal your photographic supplier gives you.

*Filters.* If you have an assignment, in any format, that requires filters, check out the ones made by Tiffen and Cokin (marketed by Minolta). Both produce fine products, with filters that aid in shooting about any assignment you can think of.

*Background Paper.* Background paper provides a colorful background for just about any type of shoot you'll be doing. The paper comes in rolls that are 9 or 12 feet wide, in colors ranging from blue, white, and gray, to the more complex colors of the spectrum. The company that makes the background paper most photographers select is Savage.

## GETTING EQUIPMENT FOR NOTHING

It isn't always true that if you get something for nothing, it can't be any good, especially when you're talking about Canon Professional Service and Nikon Professional Service.

Both Canon and Nikon maintain an inventory of equipment that they lend on a regular basis to working, professional photographers. So, if for instance you have an assignment that requires a lens that is not in your equipment arsenal, you can write to Nikon Professional Service or Canon Professional Service to borrow one.

Of course, NPS only lends Nikon equipment, while CPS only lends Canon equipment. Let me emphasize the fact that *only* Canon and Nikon perform this service for the professional photographer.

Olympus does not have any service like NPS or CPS, but they are making an effort to meet the needs of professional photographers.

"We're in the process of establishing a service like NPS and CPS," Jeff Richey, Olympus's Photo Products Manager, told me. "We are serious about making an impact in the pro market. Any pro in need of equipment can send me tearsheets of his work to prove he's a qualified professional photographer. He can send that along with his equipment requests to me at this address: Olympus Camera Corporation, Crossways Park, Woodbury, New York 11797.

"Include a list of what you want and if the request is legitimate, we'll loan you the equipment for 90 days. One of the reasons we're doing this is to get some feedback from pros about our products and their design. You may also contact Pasquale Ferazzoli, our Director of Marketing Development, with equipment requests."

Richey sounded quite sincere in his desire to work with professional photographers. In fact, Olympus's sincerity is backed up with the relationship they have with George Kalinsky who owns his own company, Major League Graphics, Inc., based in New York City. Kalinsky and company produce the programs including photographs and graphics, for all the events at Madison Square Garden—from New York Knicks basketball to professional fights.

Kalinsky also provides the same service for the New York Mets, the New Jersey Devils, and many other professional ball clubs. In addition, he does programs for concerts—including those given by Frank Sinatra and the Rolling Stones—as well as annual reports. In short, Kalinsky is busy.

"I bought all of my camera equipment in the early '70's," Kalinsky continues. "I had Nikons, then switched to Olympus because they were the first to go with smaller cameras."

Why is Kalinsky so high on Olympus?

"If I have any problems, they bend over backwards for repairs. I wouldn't trade my relationship with them for anything. Olympus fixes things immediately. When you're a professional photographer and you're out on assignment, then come back to town for a brief time before going on the road again, you really appreciate quick repairs. I didn't have that relationship with other camera companies."

And how did Kalinsky form such a good relationship? He had had some problems with his equipment and called Olympus about getting some repairs done. From there, he developed the close, working relationship he has today.

This has led to an interesting offer. Olympus has arranged an exhibit of Kalinsky's photographs in Tokyo. After the exhibit in Tokyo, Kalinsky is thinking about having the exhibit travel to New York galleries, that are also interested in exhibiting his photographs.

All this on the basis of one phone call.

Minolta, like Olympus, does not have a specific program for dealing with professional photographers as far as the loaning of equipment is concerned. According to Rick Sammom, Vice-President of Bozell and Jacobs (Minolta's advertising agency), the decisions are made on a case-by-case basis. If you're interested in obtaining Minolta equipment for a specific assignment, you should contact Rick Sammon at Bozell and Jacobs, 6 East 43rd Street, New York, New York 10017.

The forms that follow give much of the information that would be required by the Professional Services' departments at Nikon and Canon. If you are interested in obtaining more detailed information—or applying for equipment—you can contact the companies directly (see Appendix).

**Canon** The Official 35mm Camera of the 1984 Olympic Games

CANON U.S.A., INC.
ONE CANON PLAZA, LAKE SUCCESS, N.Y. 11042
TELEPHONE: (516) 488-6700
TELEX NO: 96-1333 CABLE: CANONUSA LAKS

Dear Professional Photographer:

Canon U.S.A., INC. presently offers Canon Professional Services (CPS) designed for full time professional photographers. CPS has been established to enable Canon U.S.A., INC. to supply the professional with equipment for the following purposes:

- Testing equipment for special assignments.
- Temporary replacements when photographer's equipment is in need of major repair.

Eligibility in CPS requires that sufficient evidence substantiating your professional status be submitted. All applicants must provide the following items:

1. Letter of introduction from applicant on company letterhead, stating:
   A. Position within company where presently employed,
   B. home address and phone number,
   C. type of equipment owned.
2. Two passport type head and shoulders photographs of applicant.

In addition, the following items are required depending on the nature of employment.

I. <u>Working Press</u>
   1. Three recent tearsheets with photo credits.
   2. Copy of current press credentials.
   3. A letter from your editor or bureau chief stating your position on staff.

II. <u>Freelance</u>
   1. Six recent tear sheets with photo credit or other evidence of publication.
   2. Two letters from clients stating that they have used your photographic services.
   3. Copies of membership cards from photo organizations (if applicable).
   4. Copies of press passes (if applicable).

III. <u>Commercial/Studio</u>
   1. Samples of studio letterhead, brochures and price lists.
   2. Three samples of recent work.
   3. Two letters from clients stating that they have used your photographic services.
   4. Copies of membership cards from photo organizations (if applicable).

IV <u>Corporate</u>
   1. Letter from supervisor/department head stating your position on staff.
   2. Copy of company I.D.
   3. Three samples of your work.
   4. Copies of membership cards from photo organizations (if applicable).

(continued on page 2)

*This letter sets forth the eligibility requirements for Canon's Professional Service.*

-2-

V Government/Education
1. Letter from supervisor/department head stating your position on staff.
2. Copy of company I.D.
3. Three samples of your work (if applicable).
4. Copies of membership cards from photo organizations (if applicable).

VI Miscellaneous
Please send as much of above listed credentials as available.

After these credentials are received and certified your membership will be finalized and a copy of the application along with our CPS membership card will be issued to you. When your registration is complete you can place a loan request by contacting our Headquarter's office at 516-488-6700, or outside New York state call 800-645-8188, Extension 3350 or 3351.

Canon's Professional Loan Program is for the purposes outlined above and neither to be used for the replacement of personal equipment, nor to be rendered as a permanent loan for any service considerations, testimonials, etc. All loans are on a short term basis, generally for a 14 day period, and are on a first come-first serve basis.

Additionally, membership into CPS will help you obtain priority repair service. You will also receive Canon's Professional Newsletter, THE PRO-FILE periodically.

For further information on CPS, please contact Judy Habert or Lisa Marie Saladino. For any technical assistance, please feel free to contact our National Technical Department.

We look forward to the opportunity to work with you and to show you the advantages of the Canon Photographic System.

Sincerely,

Canon Professional Loan Service
National Technical Department
Photographic Products Division

**Canon**

| FOR OFFICE USE | |
|---|---|
| CPS # ____ | Status ____ |
| Date Issued ____ | ____ |
| Expiration Date ____ | ____ |
| | ____ |
| Authorization: | |

Canon U.S.A., Inc.
National Technical Department
1 Canon Plaza
Lake Success, New York 11042
Tel: (516) 488-6700

**CANON PROFESSIONAL SERVICES**

NAME ____ PHONE NO. ____

ADDRESS ____ CITY ____ STATE ____ ZIP ____

COMPANY NAME ____ PHONE NO. ____

ADDRESS ____ CITY ____ STATE ____ ZIP ____

## CPS LOAN APPLICATION

In order to induce Canon U.S.A., Inc. (herein after "Canon") to permit me to participate in its Professional Loan Program, I agree to the following:

1. I will notify Canon in writing in the event of any change of my address or of my employment. Street addresses must be supplied. All shipments will be made to my business address unless specified for home delivery.
2. Equipment loaned to me will be kept at my address as filed with Canon except when such equipment is in actual use by me on location. All equipment shall be returned within the period of time stated on the Loan Shipping Order which accompanies the loan equipment. This equipment is not to be considered as a permanent loan. It is intended solely for my personal use and I will not lend the equipment to any other person. Failure to return the loaned equipment on time will result in Canon's invoicing me for the full value of the loaned items at the then current dealer net price and I agree to pay said invoice within thirty (30) days of receipt of the same.
3. I will carry all risk insurance on all equipment loaned to me. Such insurance shall list Canon as a co-insured, I also agree to reimburse Canon for the cost of any repairs neccessitated due to mis-handling, carelessness or neglect of the equipment while on loan. I will not be responsible however for ordinary wear. I agree to reimburse Canon for any loss, theft, or mysterious disappearance of equipment on loan to me in the event such loss is not reimbursed to Canon under the all risk insurance policy. I will forward to Canon a copy of any report submitted to the pertinent police department in the event of loss, theft or mysterious disappearance.
4. I recognize that Canon reserves the right to recall any item of equipment on five (5) days' prior written notice mailed to me at the address in effect at the time of the loan. Quantities are limited and are available on a first come - first serve basis.
5. The registration card issued to me and any equipment loaned to me are not transferrable. All equipment will be returned by me to the Canon office from which such equipment had been loaned.
6. I will promptly notify Canon of the loss of my registration card and complete such forms as may be required by Canon for the issuance of a new card.
7. I understand that all loan requests will be reviewed by Canon and Canon will determine priority and scheduling of loans in its sole and absolute discretion. The registration cards issued to me will be effective for an initial period of one year, and if renewed, for a further period of two years.

I agree to the above stated terms and further acknowledge that Canon may cancel my Professional registration and all professional privileges afforded by Canon at any time, at its discretion.

*I understand my responsibilities regarding the Canon merchandise listed on the Loan Shipping Order, and I will personally guarantee the return of this merchandise, or payment for any part not returned, when recalled by the Canon Technical Department.*

____ Signature ____ Date

*Here is a Canon Professional Services loan application. It sets forth the terms of the loan of the equipment.*

**Canon**
PROFESSIONAL SERVICES
Membership Card

PHOTO

______________________________

CPS #________Exp. Date.______

______________________________

*Signature* This card is non-transferable.

CANON U.S.A., INC.
Lake Success NY 11042 516/488-6700

CANON PROFESSIONAL SERVICES MEMBERSHIP CARD

NAME______________________________

CPS #____________________

ISSUE DATE________________EXP. DATE.________

AUTHORIZED BY______________________________

*This is a copy of the Canon Professional Services card, that every CPS member gets after joining.*

You *must* fully complete this questionnaire for approval.
Incomplete questionnaires will not be processed.

NPS

# NIKON PROFESSIONAL SERVICES

## INVITATION TO JOIN

"I AM AN ACTIVE, FULL-TIME PROFESSIONAL NIKON PHOTOGRAPHER" and herewith apply for membership to Nikon Professional Services.

NAME__________ AGE_____ BIRTHDATE__________

COMPANY __________ SOC. SEC. # __________

ADDRESS __________

CITY__________ STATE__________ ZIP__________

PHONE NO. (AREA CODE) __________

HOME ADDRESS __________

CITY__________ STATE__________ ZIP__________

PHONE NO. (AREA CODE) __________

Mailing address preferred ☐ home ☐ office

My work involves the following areas:

( ) Photojournalism/Sports ( ) Advertising/Illustration/AV
( ) Commercial/Studio ( ) in-plant industrial ( ) Medical/Scientific
( ) Forensic ( ) Other—please specify __________

I use the following Nikon equipment: ( ) owned by me ( ) company supplied

NPS Sponsor __________ NPS # __________

Sponsor Signature __________

## QUALIFICATION REQUIREMENT

**I am a member in good standing of the following organization(s):**

☐ NPPA ☐ PP of A ☐ ASMP ☐ other __________

Please give Membership No. __________

**You must submit the following:** 1. Company letterhead or business card of the company who employs you as a professional photographer; 2. If self-employed, your own business card and letterhead; 3. Two examples (tear sheets) of your most recently published work.

**Credit Reference:**

NAME __________ COMPANY __________

ADDRESS __________ PHONE ( ) __________

I understand that the rapid repair feature of the Nikon Professional Services is available to me on Nikon equipment only. I understand and agree to waive the usual estimate procedure on any rapid repairs I may have in the interest of time. I will to the best of my ability follow Nikon instructions for packing and insuring any equipment I return for repairs.

**I agree to be fully responsible for any equipment borrowed from NPS and assume all risks and hazards until such equipment is returned and received by NPS. I further agree that title to such equipment is and shall remain the property of Nikon and that I shall indemnify and pay Nikon for any loss or damage to such equipment.**

☞ Signed__________ Date __________

FOR OFFICE USE

Professional affiliation verified   Employment verified   NPS No. Assigned

*This is a copy of the Nikon Professional Service form. It also lists the qualifications necessary for the loan of equipment.*

## CHAPTER EIGHT

# CHOOSING YOUR "SPACE"

Once you have your equipment, you're going to need some place to put it. There used to be an old radio show called "Fibber McGee and Molly." They were a rather domestic couple who had this incredible closet. Every week, McGee would open that closet and out would come everything from Roman chariots to old tennis rackets. If you don't want to be like McGee, that is, storing your equipment in some closet until you need it, you're going to have to select the proper space for your studio.

### DEFINING YOUR NEEDS

The type of space you select will depend upon the type of work you're going to be doing. Eventually, if your business is profitable, you can expand. But your immediate concern is what kind of space you'll need *now*.

In addition to considering the type of work you're doing, another major consideration is whether or not you will be doing your own processing. Some photographers like to have a lab on premises so they can do their own printing and processing. One school of thought says that if you do your own processing, you have final control over the way your prints and slides will look. Another school of thought says that a photographer doesn't get paid for printing and processing; he gets paid for taking pictures.

In this instance, there's no right or wrong way to go. I think, though, that if you could find a lab that does your printing and processing exactly to your specifications, it pays to let them do this work. This will leave you more time to concentrate on the process of photography.

Another consideration as to the type of space to buy or rent is how much can you afford? If you are setting up your business in a rural area, where space is not at a premium, your cost to rent or buy space is going to be less. A photographer who is renting or buying space in an urban area where space is at a premium will no doubt pay more.

This doesn't mean, however, that just because space is cheaper in a rural area, that's where you should open your business. You'll have more photographic opportunities, that is, the opportunity to break into a variety of photographic categories (as outlined in chapter two) in a more urban area. Just keep in mind, the denser the population, the more the space will cost you.

*Buying or renting.* The ideal situation when you're starting out in business is to rent with an option to buy. This gives you more capital to put into the day-to-day running of the business, including cost of equipment, film, etc.

If you can't get an option to buy, your only other choices are to buy outright or rent. Let's look at these options.

If you buy outright, you'll be your own landlord and responsible for the upkeep of the premises. Any repairs to the facilities—plumbing, electrical, or structural—will come out of your own pocket. You'll also be limited in terms of changing location unless you can sell your space and move easily. Selling space can be a long and lengthy process involving real estate brokers and lawyers.

However, for all its drawbacks, if your business isn't under-capitalized, it's nice to be your own landlord and own your own space. It gives you a legitimate investment in your future. And, if you've located in an area that is economically thriving, chances are the value of your property will go up, so when you do decide to sell, you'd make a profit.

One of the biggest drawbacks to renting space is that you're at the whim of the landlord. According to the lease you sign, he may be obligated to make repairs, and give necessary heat in the winter, but have you ever tried to enforce those provisions against a landlord who's trying to make money by cutting your services? Depending upon where you live, there may be state or city agencies to help you with a grievance with a landlord, but until an agreement is reached, or adjudicated in a court should it become necessary, you're going to be miserable.

What I've just described is, admittedly, a worse case scenario, but you might as well be aware of it. The way, however, to try and avoid something like this happening, is to make sure that you sign a *lease* before renting any space.

So, if you're renting, read the lease carefully before signing it. If there's something you don't understand, get a friend who's a lawyer, and not a friend who *sounds* like a lawyer, to read the lease. If you don't have a friend who's a lawyer, pay for one, even if it costs a $100 fee for the lawyer's time. If you want certain provisions in the lease, make sure you spell them out in writing, attach them as an addendum to the lease, and get the landlord to sign or initial that addendum, as well as the lease itself. Finally, *always* keep a signed copy for yourself.

## TYPES OF SPACE

After considering whether to buy or rent, your next decision is what kind of space you're going to need. Here are the most common types of space that photographers in my acquaintance have opted for.

*The Office.* Much of the public's conception of a photographer is a fellow with jazzy clothes, surrounded by gorgeous models, who has a great time shooting in his spacious studio in the middle of glamorous Manhattan. That is simply the media's generalized conception of how and where a photographer works.

Many photographers who do not do studio work very often prefer an office from which to conduct business. Photojournalists, corporate (annual report), and photographers specializing in editorial illustration can do their work nicely from an office. After all, they are going to be on location most of the time. There's no necessity to have studio space unless they are going to be doing studio work as well.

If you are going to be on location a lot, you'll need an office with enough room for desk, filing cabinets, typewriter (on which you'll type invoices to clients), storage space for equipment, and maybe a lab if you're doing your own processing.

*The House.* Some photographers begin conducting business from their house, doing their studio work there, and then move into more formal quarters.

You can conduct a very nice wedding, portrait or commercial business if you have either a separate wing of your house or a completely finished basement that's been turned into a studio. You'll also need adjoining space for an adequate reception area, and a separate room to use as an office where you can have complete privacy.

The biggest drawback from a professional point-of-view to using your house as a studio is that the clients you are dealing with, either the wedding and portrait trade, or more commercially-oriented clients like art directors, might perceive you as being a little less than a professional because you're doing work in the informal environment of home.

When people pay money for a product, they expect the trappings. Remember, they've seen photographers like Scavullo profiled on TV, and they think that if you're a professional, you have to have a professional looking space. No matter how good you are as a photographer, they may not take you seriously if you're photographing them or their products in your home.

Only you can make the decision as to whether to do your business at home or select a separate space. You can begin at home, see how things go, and if you don't get any negative feedback from clients, stay with the home environment. If you do get the negative feedback, it may be time to look into a different type of space as an alternative.

*Storefront Studio.* This sounds like the name of a new TV show. "Storefront Studio," a comedy about the people who work in and hang around a photographer's storefront studio. No, you can't steal my idea. I've already copyrighted it (see chapter 8)!

Actually, many photographers going into business elect to open up a storefront studio. Usually, they will be dealing with the public a lot. This includes wedding and portrait photographers (who may also be doing studio commercial work if they have enough space), team and school photographers, and in some smaller areas, commercial photographers.

For the wedding, portrait, school, and team photographers, the storefront studio gives them instant access to their customers. All they have to do is walk in. In the storefront space, the potential client will usually find a reception area, a camera room where all the shooting is done, an office in the back for doing paperwork, and then a lab if the photographer is doing his own processing.

*Loft or Studio.* I've lumped the loft and studio space situations into one category because they are essentially the same: a separate space, away from the general public, where the photographer does his work.

Such a space is usually located in a large building that is zoned for business purposes, though this may not always be the case. In New York, in particular, photographers have been fighting for years over whether their lofts in buildings are businesses or personal residences, especially considering that many photographers in this situation have an adjoining living space.

The photographic categories that fall into the loft/studio space are commercial, advertising, fashion, and catalogue. Some corporate photographers also maintain studio space so they can do portfolio work and occasional commercial assignments.

In the loft/studio, there's a separate reception area when a client arrives. Adjacent is the shooting area which is usually quite large. Depending on the construction of the building, there might be large, bay windows to admit light, so you have the option of using natural or artificial light on an assignment. Commercial photographer Pete Turner has this type of lighting set-up.

Another photographer I know, Lou Jawitz, has a large, beautiful skylight, that admits a soft, diffuse light into his studio. This gives him the option of using natural or ambient light, artificial light, or a combination of the two.

In addition to the shooting area, there's a separate office, and maybe a lab. I've also seen duplex arrangements, where one floor is living and storage quarters, while another floor is the shooting space, reception area, and office. How much space you buy or rent depends on whether you'll be living on premises or not, how much space you'll need for the volume of work you'll be doing and, of course, how much money you can afford to rent or buy the space.

I should also mention that photographers tend to store the bulk of their equipment, including cameras, lights, and background paper in or near the shooting area for easy access. Since many commercial photographers also have to build sets for "shoots" themselves, or send out such assignments to set makers, they make sure that the shooting area is large enough to accommodate these set requirements. There may also be a separate space to store props.

Also, make sure that the electrical wiring can handle the type of equipment you'll be using—especially if you will be using more than one light bank at a time. There should also be proper ventilation and plumbing available for use if you decide you want on-site processing.

## RECEPTION AREA

Regardless of the type of photography business you've established, it's important to have a reception area where a client can wait comfortably.

The best reception area I've ever seen was in fashion photographer Jan Cobb's studio. It was far enough away from the shooting area to provide the guest with some privacy. In it, Cobb had placed a VCR and a generous selection of pre-recorded videotapes. This way, in case he couldn't see a client for awhile, the client could put on a videotape and be amused in the interim.

## GENERALIZED COSTS

I say generalized, because it's impossible to give you specifics in this area. It all depends on which area of the country you'll be shooting in.

In general, the loft/studio will cost you the most amount of money. Since they are usually located in an urban area where space is at a premium, they cost the most. For instance, in Manhattan, where the largest amount of commercial photographers in the country are congregated, a typical studio space of 1200 square feet runs about $2000 a month and more.

A storefront studio, though, can be just as high. One New York photographer told me that a storefront wedding studio on Northern Boulevard in the borough of Queens (part of New York City), runs as high as $5,000 a month. This studio is considerably smaller than the average commercial one I just mentioned. The reason the rent is so high is because of the location: Northern Boulevard is a heavily traveled thoroughfare.

Certainly, the cost of renting an office or using a portion of your house for business will be considerably less than renting a loft/studio or storefront studio. You won't be renting as much space, and you probably will not be located in a dense, commercially-zoned area. Of course, you could have an office in a dense area. But, since you won't need that much space, the rent, when compared to the other space options, will be less.

In terms of buying space, once again it'll depend on real estate values in your area, which in turn depend upon whether space is at a premium or maximum. For instance, buying a storefront studio in a rural area will cost considerably less than the $100,000 mark which you could use as a minimum price to buy a moderate sized studio in a large city like New York, Chicago, or Los Angeles.

If you want to buy a loft/studio, they're into the hundreds of thousands of dollars in these same, large urban areas. And don't forget the maintenance costs which can run into the thousands each month. This is why photographers, when they are first starting out, generally *rent* with one or more photographers until they can afford to buy or rent on their own.

Houses, of course, depend on the area of the country where you'll be working. For example, you can't touch a moderate sized house in an economically thriving part of the Los Angeles metropolitan area for under $250,000. The same amount of space in the New York area would run a minimum of $100,000 less.

*Making a choice.* Unless you can really afford it, rent. If you make the money later on so you can buy, then buy. But whatever you do, don't strap yourself. Don't give yourself the added burden of paying rent or maintenance costs on a space that you really can't afford. All that will happen is your business will go under. Fast.

## PHOTOGRAPHERS AND SPACE

What kind of space do some photographers utilize? How do space considerations work in actual practice? Consider the situations of the following photographers.

*Rudy Pollak—Wedding Photography.* Pollak is a dapper, well-spoken wedding and portrait photographer, who has a studio (Dino Custom Color Photography Studio) in Elmhurst, New York.

"We really do a lot of different types of work, besides portraits and weddings," Pollak adds. "Last week, I had a woman come into the studio (it's a storefront) who had been beaten up by her husband. There was a court case pending and she needed a picture for her lawyers of her bruised face."

While the above instance is rare, Pollak is a generalist, who also shoots pictures of dogs, cats, and occasional product shots.

"My studio measures 18 feet by 45 feet. When you first come in, there's a reception area, behind that the camera room, and behind that an office for conducting business—a room where we do framing and assembly of albums, a storage room, where we also do spotting and retouching, a kitchen, and a dressing room for clients whose portraits are being taken," says Pollak.

"The shooting area is rather unique. Dino Semprini, who owned the business before I did, designed the shooting area for the angle of the lens. You see, the walls come to a point by the door, giving us the maximum amount of shooting space."

As far as the location for a wedding and portrait studio in general, Pollak suggests you make sure it's on a well-traversed thoroughfare. He also explains:

"I bought a going business that was already established, and had a reputation. I get nearly all my business from recommendations from customers, a built-in safety factor because it was, as I say, a going business when I bought it. I didn't have to worry about building up my initial trade, and I'd advise anyone going into the wedding and portrait business to buy a business that's already established, if you can."

As to how much money he makes a year, Pollak reveals, "I make a living. We're basically a 'mom and pop' studio that does quality work. That's the difference: there are some studios that are literally wedding factories. They turn 'em out and lose quality. It's two different roads for the wedding and portrait photographer entering the business to follow: do quality or become a factory and lose quality."

Adds Mary Semprini, who with her husband Dino were the first owners of the Dino Custom Color Photography Studio:

"You have to know your craft. Today, there aren't too many craftsmen, people who are willing to put in the time to do quality work. And you have to like people. People are 90% of your business."

*Alan Zenreich—Still Life/Special Effects Photography.* Alan Zenreich is a still life/special effects photographer, who shares his studio space with another photographer, on Fifth Avenue off 13th Street in Manhattan.

Zenreich specializes in doing commercial work, but has editorial accounts as well.

"My studio space measures 1200 square feet, plus we have 13 foot ceilings which makes it easy when we raise lights on light stands during a shoot. Let's face it, with the high cost of renting studio space in Manhattan, a photographer has no choice but to share," Zenreich says.

"I find," he continues, "that money goes out . . . *ad infinitum,* to pay for this or that. Our rent here is $2000 a month, not to mention the costs of phone and electric. And, when you're first starting in business, you also have to give the electric and phone companies a deposit."

Zenreich's studio space is organized. When you get off the elevator, a reception area is available with couches and tables with current magazines. After going through a connecting door, you arrive in the camera room filled with all kinds of equipment, including cameras, lights, and rolls of background paper. When not in use, they are neatly placed against the sides of the studio. In back is Zenreich's lab. He's one of those who prefers doing his own printing and processing.

"It's part of being a professional photographer to run your own film," he says emphatically.

Next to the lab is a kitchen and a bathroom. But what makes his studio really unique is what a first-time visitor usually misses. If you go through the door on your left when you come off the elevator, you'll be in Zenreich's office, which has a complete computer set-up. His entire business is computerized, and he's a specialist in combining computer graphics with live action photography. In fact, he's so good at integrating computers into a photographer's business, both artistically and as a solid business practice, i.e., generating invoices every month to clients who owe him money, that Zenreich is in constant demand to talk before photography organizations about his specialty.

"I am a mechanic," he concludes. "Professionals have to have not only all the tools at their disposal to do their job, but the knowledge and ability to use them properly.

*Burt Glinn—Annual Report/Corporate Photography.* Burt Glinn, the photojournalist turned corporate photographer, maintains a small suite of offices off Central Park West in New York City.

His offices are located in an apartment building with a doorman to give the place the character that *any* Central Park West space should have, per the requirements of New York City security purposes and what the general public thinks a Central Park West space should be like.

When you come into Glinn's offices, you're in a small room. On either wall are make-shift tables on which magazines, brochures, and annual reports to which Glinn has contributed are stacked. In the middle of the room is a desk from which Glinn does his business. Behind him is a smaller area that contains filing cabinets filled with photographs and slides. There's also room to view slides on a carousel projector.

In the back is a storage area. Since Glinn is frequently on the road, he has little reason to maintain, or pay for, a large amount of space, like any successful photographer, who's a good businessman.

*Don Banks—Commercial Photography.* Don Banks the commercial photographer who specializes in bookcover photography, has one of the more ingenious shooting spaces I've ever seen. As a bookcover photographer, he shoots in his apartment, which overlooks the East River.

When you enter Banks' apartment, you pass through a foyer lined with stunning photographs from previous shoots. If you go to your left, you come to a combination dressing, make-up, and filing room. Here Banks has set up mirrors for use by the models he works with. He also has, on the side, cabinets where he stores his slides and a light box.

Banks is also a whiz at graphic design, and the room shows this. Everything seems in harmony here, despite so many disparate elements that include the following: a fishtank where he keeps exotic fish; an aquarium where he keeps Gekos; and separate table where he's placed his Rollodex and phone. And also on the side, is a complete file of male and female models from the large New York City modeling agencies. This way, when Banks needs a model for a shoot, he can instantly thumb through the files and pick one.

As far as the shooting area is concerned, that's out the door and to the left. In the shooting area, there are large windows that admit light that can be used for a shoot. Or, Banks can set up his lights. There's also room for the wonderfully imaginative sets he builds himself, or hires a set builder or model maker to do instead.

Next to the shooting area is the kitchen. One of the things Banks has done to help his business, as well as his eating habits, is to hire Emilio, a chef/houseboy. This gives Banks the freedom to do what he does best, photography. Meanwhile, Emilio keeps things shipshape around the studio, including cooking gourmet meals that clients love. In fact, Banks thinks Emilio's culinary talents, as well as his own photographic ones, have induced clients to give him more business. They love Emilio's cooking and how many photographers do you know who have enough class to employ a gourmet cook?

Rounding out Banks' apartment set-up is a bathroom and a bedroom. All-in-all a convenient way to do business.

*Steve Grohe—Advertising Photography.* I talked about Steve Grohe and his work in large format in the previous chapter, but let's look at his studio space for a moment.

Grohe maintains a studio in downtown Boston, Massachusetts. It's 5,000 square feet that occupies two floors, including reception and shooting areas, and a lab that he uses to process an occasional black-and-white shot. The rest of the time he sends his Ektachrome 200 out to a lab to be processed.

Because of his large studio space, Grohe is free to construct elaborate sets.

"We do a lot of set building," Grohe confirms. "It's something I especially enjoy doing. I once designed a 1903 French airship for a shoot. I then rented it out to one of the TV stations up here and made some extra money," he recalls with amusement.

*Daniel Aubrey—Travel Photography.* Daniel Aubrey has probably the most interesting background of any photographer I've ever met. He was a Hollywood screenwriter before turning to photography.

Among his many professional writing assignments was the screenplay for the film *El Cid,* that starred Charlton ("Mr. Wood") Heston and Sophia Loren.

Aubrey turned to photography because he loves making photographs. He specializes in doing travel photographs for airline magazines and other publications that print photographs from exotic places. At the time we spoke, Aubrey was particularly delighted because he'd "broken" into *Travel and Leisure* magazine.

As far as studio space is concerned, he works out of a brownstone on New York's eastside. On one floor he has his living space and in the back is a file room where he sorts slides for assignments, and maintains stock files. Aubrey also sells his photographs as stock whenever possible. On a lower floor is a small studio which he shares with a commercial photographer. Aubrey has been branching out into commercial and corporate work, and likes the option of having a studio on premises to do his commercial work as well as to shoot photographs to add to his portfolio.

# CHAPTER NINE

# PROMOTING THE BUSINESS

Contacts are the single most important facet of a photographer's business. Without contacts; he'll starve. How do you form contacts that lead to photographic assignments? You begin with a list.

## THE CONTACT LIST

This could also be referred to as the "hit" list, but your weapon is going to be a phone rather than a .44 Magnum. And you better feel lucky because you're about to meet your public. A contact list is a carefully thought out list of potential clients. It can be organized in three ways.

Contact List A is a list of the job contacts you already have in your personal address book or Rollodex. These contacts are individuals who you've already done business with, or who have shown enough previous interest in your work that with little or no effort, you can show them your portfolio.

Contact List B is a list of potential clients; people that you have no previous association with but who might be interested in your services. Depending on the category of photography you're in, you could conceivably have quite a varied list.

For instance, a commercial photographer might have on his Contact List B the art director of an advertising agency that uses still lifes in its ads. He may also include a photography magazine that does layouts of the work of professional photographers; another magazine in the general interest area that sometimes hires photographers to create covers for them; and so forth.

Contact List B will be the most creative, the most outlandish contact list you'll put together. Anyone and everyone you think you can sell your work to should be on it. You should then take the time to whittle it down to the most promising contacts which should be "hit" first.

The third list, Contact List C, is a list of relatives. As with financing for business, relatives can also be overlooked as business contacts. For instance, if you have a cousin in the real estate business, he's probably employing a photographer to shoot the photographs for his real estate listings. So, why shouldn't he employ you to shoot those photographs, assuming you have the skills, instead of some stranger?

## SELLING YOURSELF

The contact list is complete, and you begin the business of selling yourself to potential clients. Making a good impression is imperative. This is another instance where your previous evaluation of your strengths and weaknesses can be helpful.

*Phone Manner.* Much of your business is going to be done over the phone. It is the single, most effective way to schedule an appointment with a client. The problem is clients usually prefer initial communication by letter. They don't want to be bothered by some stranger on the telephone. Yet, for the photographer, it's much easier to sell the client over the phone than any other way. And when I say selling, I don't mean that you're going to get a job. That's possible, but what you want to do is simply generate enough interest that the person on the other end of the line wants to see your portfolio. In a way, he matches up those images to an image of the person he gets from your initial conversation.

The key is projecting your personality through Mr. Bell's invention. Most people have trouble doing that. Put a phone in front of them, and it's like speaking into a microphone, with a coast-to-coast hook-up—they become stiff and awkward.

So how do you project your personality over the phone? You have to relax. It's the only way your natural, effervescent, ebullient, likable, and all-American personality will come across. Remember, you're not just selling photographs; on a very real level, you're selling yourself. If you're a good salesman, you'll have no difficulty getting jobs.

How do you relax? The methods are as varied as people. Some like to do deep-breathing exercises. Others do something physical, like smoking a cigarette, chug-a-lugging coffee or exercising to work off nervous tension.

But aside from any of these things, when you're making a phone call to a contact, especially a "cold" one, it's frightening. No one wants to be summarily rejected. It can literally be overwhelming when a potential client says to you over the phone, "Not interested."

So in addition to doing something tangible that relaxes you, you should psych yourself up so that the possibility of rejection, which is always present, does not dominate your thoughts. If it does, the person on the other end of the line will sense your desperation and may choose not to do business with you because you're making *them* feel uncomfortable.

Before a phone call to a potential client, I like to say to myself, 'You know, Fred, he's not the only fish in the ocean,' no matter how desperate I feel for work that day. What I convince myself of is that he needs me as much as I need him. More often than not, this type of psyching works.

Sometimes, though, this attitude isn't successful. While I relax and control the flow of conversation, I can come across as arrogant, not confident, which has lost me jobs. No matter what techniques get you through the trauma of the phone call, you must come across as confident, but without alienating the other person. If you can do this, you'll be able with ease to set up an appointment to show your portfolio to a potential client. You might also want to write out your telephone "pitch" beforehand rather than trying to ad-lib once you've made contact. If you deliver the written copy with a nice, easy cadence, you can be very persuasive. Many companies that solicit phone sales have salesmen use this method when contacting potential customers.

One final point about your phone manner. It's essential that you address the contact by his or her first name. Immediately, it establishes in their minds that you are equals. Had you addressed them by the formal appellation of "Mr." or "Ms.," they would have the choice of whether or not to be familiar and address you by your first name. So, they're "Mr.," and you're "Joe." So, try not to let the client get one up on you, at least until they're giving you lucrative assignments.

*Clothing.* Do you remember elementary school assembly? One day each week, you had to come to school wearing a certain "uniform." In my school it was black pants, white shirt and a red snapping tie that crossed at the middle. (They never mentioned shoes, so I guess they were optional.)

The point is, if you dressed the way the school wanted, you didn't have any trouble. If you didn't, you got a demerit. Enough demerits and your parents were called. The question became whether or not you expressed your individuality by wearing a plaid shirt, or you played the game and dressed like everyone else, while thinking whatever you wanted.

This situation is analogous to the way you present yourself when you see a potential client for the first time. If you dress with leather pants and work shirt, you'll be perceived as being flamboyant, which in some conservative business minds implies you're not serious enough to do the job. Why take the chance of forming a negative image?

"When a photographer comes in to see me with his portfolio, I don't want to see him dress like a hippie," says Virginia Murphy-Hamill, director of design for Hearst Business Communications. "I know photographers are creative people, but if they dress like a hippie, they won't look professional. No dungarees and earring through the ear.

"A suit isn't necessary either. If a photographer dresses neatly, with a collared shirt and maybe a sweater, sort of Ivy League, that's fine."

*Interpersonal Communication.* There are a number of reasons why one photographer gets the job while another does not. It all comes down to interpersonal communication.

Few of us bother to listen to the person speaking. We may be off someplace else in our minds, concentrating on something else. When an important question is put to us, like "What is your photographic specialty?", the tendency is to stutter, and you wind up losing the job because you couldn't even express yourself.

Pay attention. You're there to get a client. Listen to what he has to say. Concentrate and answer intelligently. If you're only addressing one person, which in communications rhetoric is called a dyad, you should have no problem keeping the conversation flowing. If another person is brought in to see your work, for example, the art director brings in an agency account executive, you have one more person to direct your attention to.

When dealing with two persons, don't stiffen up and feel it's two against one. Remember, you're their equal and act it. Just make certain that you don't ignore either of the other two in your conversation.

Recently, I was in a situation where I had been hired to write an article about the use of a new piece of photographic machinery. The weather was humid; I was late for my appointment. I was wearing my suit, Brontosaurus tie knotted. I began to run to make the appointment.

When I showed up, my contact ushered me into an antiseptic conference room. By this time, I was sweating from the run I'd just made. Then, an agency vice-president entered the room.

Great. There I am, sweating onto my note pad, thinking what a lousy impression I'm making, and not *listening* to them. Then I remembered I was a freelancer—that my life didn't depend on this job. I got a hold of myself, and went to the bathroom to wash up. When I came back, I took off my jacket, opened my tie like *Harry O*, (remember the fine actor, David Janssen) and said, "Let's get down to business."

They loved it. I *listened* to what both men had to say, responded in kind, and they were impressed with the article I subsequently wrote.

The point is that I was honest, and I listened. Despite a tepid beginning, things worked out.

A moment ago I talked about listening. It's a dying art. More jobs are lost because the photographer just doesn't understand what the art director, editor, or client is looking for. If you practice listening skills with personal friends before going into the interview, you'll be attuned to listening and thinking about your reply at the same time. It's a handy skill to have. Some people refer to it as "thinking on your feet."

There's one other point you should be aware of, which is that potential clients want you to be realistic about your abilities, and not try to con them. Pat Perry of *The Saturday Evening Post* magazine cites this example.

"A few weeks ago, I had two local photographers come in looking for a job shooting for the magazine. Their expectations were unrealistic. Neither of them had enough experience or a portfolio that demonstrated the range of their photographic capabilities.

"But what they really lacked was the objectivity to realize all of this. I wondered about how much work they had actually done. I recommended that they build up their experience and portfolio by getting into local contests, competitions, house organs of large corporations. This way, they'd develop the talent to deal with all kinds of photographic situations, which is something I look for in any photographer I hire to do a shoot for our magazine."

*Accepting and using criticism.* "You know, if someone's stuff doesn't get used, they shouldn't take it personally. Their work is being evaluated, not the person," says Steve Pollock of *Popular Photography* magazine.

Pollock makes a point that should be stressed—if you don't get the job, *you're* not being rejected, the work is. The photographer, like any creative individual, has to be able to separate himself, his identity, from his work. While the work is a representation of his identity, there are other things that go into the making of a person's soul. To forget that is to deny yourself the opportunity to learn from constructive criticism.

Notice I say constructive. There are plenty of people out there who will criticize your work because it makes them feel good to take somebody else down simply because they have such a poor opinion of themselves. Occasionally, you're going to run into this kind of person.

When someone criticizes your work, take it from whom it comes. If you honestly feel the person is trying to hurt you, tell yourself they're behaving unbusinesslike and forget it. But have the objectivity to consider what the potential client is saying. More often than not, they're going to be trying to help you.

Even when Pat Perry constructively criticized those two photographers, he was, at the same time, giving them suggestions on improving their presentation. If they had been listening, they also would have heard Perry offer the advice to try and get into one of the stock photo agencies, like Gamma/Liason in New York or the Picture Group in Rhode Island.

*Other Selection Criteria.* Besides being a good communicator and a good photographer, what else do potential clients look for? Flexibility, both financially and photographically.

Clients want to know that the photographer they're hiring is versatile, and that he can work in more than one photographic format should the need arise. At the same time, they want to work with a photographer who doesn't value his abilities to the point where he prices himself out of business.

You should always get a fair return for your time, and the ASMP (American Society of Magazine Photographers) in New York has some very good guidelines on pricing your work. But you should be flexible regardless. "I want to work with photographers who are willing to negotiate," Pat Perry emphasizes.

Of course, the photographer will be trying to cut the best deal possible for himself, and so will the client. But if *both* of you aren't flexible enough to understand the other's needs—what kind of a budget the client has for the shoot versus the amount of time, effort, and cost of materials on the photographer's end—then a fair agreement will not be reached. So as long as you're not compromising yourself or your work, try to be flexible.

## NETWORKING CONTACTS

The idea behind networking is that every contact has a contact of their own. By getting in "good" with the first contact, you then get the opportunity to ask the first contact to introduce you to a second one, which can lead to a third, a fourth, and so on.

The two photographers who spoke to Pat Perry weren't even in good, yet they were still getting an opportunity to network. What Perry told them was the benefits of *his* networking. He explains, with the following example.

"Last week, we had to find a photographer in Washington, D.C. to do some portraits for us. Now I knew of one photographer there, but for a variety of reasons, I decided not to use him. Instead, I went to two stock agencies that also employ photographers to go out on separate shoots: Gamma/Liason out of New York and the Picture Group out of Rhode Island. Both agencies have their own network of photographers they work with. I trust them. They work with good ones.

"I had to be assured they were good because it was an important assignment. We wound up using a photographer from the Picture Group and we were satisfied with the work."

There's nothing to stop you from asking an art director, magazine editor, or any potential client if they could give you a recommendation to someone they think can use your services. That's how you network. Just ask. Sometimes, you may run into someone like Virginia Murphy-Hamill who does the networking for you.

"On occasion, I've seen photographers whose work didn't fit into the magazines I'm working on. For instance, I don't use fashion shots, but in my freelance work I sometimes have occasion to use a freelance fashion photographer. So I'd keep the person with the fashion shots in mind.

"If I can't use their work, I may also put the photographer in touch with one of my contacts who can. That's why it's a good idea when you come for the interview to give the potential client a 'leave behind piece.'

"A 'leave behind piece' is a favorite photo with the photographer's named 'knocked in' with white type. This can be done by taking a 5 × 7 photo and some black type, going to a print shop that can do this kind of work, and telling them to superimpose or 'knock out' the letters on the picture, so they come out in white. This makes a very attractive 'leave behind' that I won't easily forget."

Many art directors and editors maintain a file of the good material that's been submitted. For instance, Pat Perry keeps a regional folder of photographic submissions broken down by geographic regions for easy access.

## PROFESSIONAL CONTACTS

Another way of networking contacts is through other professional photographers. Frequently, photographers may be too busy to take all the assignments they are offered. When this happens, as in any business, they recommend other photographers for the job. How do you become one of the photographers they might recommend?

Sometimes it's as simple as doing a favor for a photographer friend that's later reciprocated. The point is to put yourself in a position where you can meet other professional photographers.

This can be done informally. For instance, in New York City, photographers like to hang out at a restaurant/bar called Joanna's. I've also seen editorial people from *Women's Wear Daily*, too. It's a good place to make the professional contacts I'm talking about.

If you want to build contacts in a more formal, structured way, consider joining one of the professional photography organizations. The three most popular ones among professional photographers are the Advertising Photographers of America (APA), the Professional Photographers of America (PPA) and the American Society of Magazine Photographers (ASMP).

*Advertising Photographers of America.* The APA was begun in 1981 by a group of independent photographers who were concerned about the future of their business. They realized the necessity of exchanging information and ideas, resolving common problems, as well as strengthening the relationships between photographers, their clients, and their suppliers. The organization grew from 50 founding members in New York City to a current membership of over 260 in New York alone. With additional chapters in Chicago, Los Angeles, and San Francisco, the nationwide membership of APA is now over 800.

APA says that their key goals are to promote the highest standards of business practice within the industry—a form of industry-wide public relations—and to promote an awareness and understanding of the role advertising photographers play within the creative community.

Aside from the networking benefits, there are other, immediately practical advantages to joining APA. They include the following:

1. The APA/SPAR Estimate/Invoice form specifically created for advertising assignments. This will help you decide on what fee to bill for a job.

2. The APA/SPAR Stock Delivery Memo and Invoice Form.

3. Invitations to four general membership meetings per year. The meetings provide a forum for discussion of problems and practices in the industry, and allow you to meet face-to-face with colleagues. It's at these meetings that you'll do most of your networking.

4. A subscription to the APA Newsletter which will help keep you informed about current APA activities as well as industry practices.

5. Use of the APA Hotline. As a member of the organization, you can call the APA office with questions or problems. The APA will try to answer questions immediately or refer you to a source that can help.

6. Free consultations with APA's legal counsel who specializes in practices of the industry and can keep you aware of legal precedents that may affect you.

7. Eligibility for APA group medical insurance. This is a subscription plan offering basic insurance plus major medical coverage, with additional dental coverage. This program can be substantially cheaper than providing your own health insurance, so it pays to check it out.

8. Eligibility for group disability income insurance coverage. Again, this can be a substantial savings, as opposed to buying individual disability insurance.

9. Discounts available when you rent cars and vans from Olins-Rent-A-Car.

10. Discounts on admissions to APA seminars.

11. Members who are assistants are entitled to a free listing in the "Assistant's Directory," published at intervals in The APA Newsletter.

12. Free promotional activities. The APA stresses that they continue to promote the role of the professional photographer in the communications industry through public relations events, editorial submissions, advertisements, trade shows, seminars, and exhibitions.

Contact the main office of the APA for other membership particulars, including the fee to join. (see Appendix)

*American Society of Magazine Photographers.* The ASMP is an organization of over 4,000 leading professional photographers in the United States and abroad. Its members work in every category of published photography—advertising, news, film and tape, and other areas including electronic impulse.

ASMP's objectives, as stated at its inception in 1944, are to safeguard and promote the interests of the photography profession; maintain and promote high professional standards and ethics in photography; cultivate friendship and mutual understanding among professional photographers.

On a practical level, ASMP's has many functions. They include:

1. Coordinating relations between members and publishers, advertising agencies, industrial firms, and other users of quality photography.

2. Helping to establish proper standards for photographers to retain ownership and resale rights to their work.

3. Instrumental influence in setting legal precedents in areas such as copyright and credit lines.

4. Working to protect photographer's rights against plagiarism and speculation.

5. Providing surveys of rates and standards for all phases of the photographer's business, including compensation, copyrights, and contracts with editors, advertising personnel, and picture agencies.

6. Offering suggested sample forms for model and property releases, assignment confirmation, and stock submissions.

ASMP has six categories of membership. Basically they are:

1. General Member—actively and professionally engaged in photography, with at least 3 years of such experience dating from published work. Their experience must consitute a majority of their total profes-

sional activity. Two sponsoring general members are required for entrance into this category.

2. Associate Member—receives all the benefits of general members, but cannot vote or hold office in the organization. This photographer may have less than 3 years experience, and entrance into this category requires one sponsoring general member.

3. Sustaining Member—receives all the benefits of a general membership, but the sustaining member cannot vote or hold office in the organization. A person who is professionally associated with photography for publication is not eligible for Associate or General membership, but can be a sustaining member. Two current general members must act as sponsors for entrance into this category.

4. Assistant Member—receives all benefits, except automatic Major Medical coverage. They also cannot vote or hold office in the organization. This member would be a current, working, full-time freelance photographic assistant. Two current General members are necessary for sponsorship.

5. Educator Member—receives all benefits, cannot vote or hold organizational office, and his application does not require sponsorship, but rather written certification of the educator's employment from his institution. This would be a photography teacher at the high school level or above, or photographic curators, researchers at libraries or schools, writers or lecturers on photographic subjects.

6. Student Member—a full-time student in the visual communications field, at college level or above, accredited by their school registrar or supervising faculty member. No sponsoring member is required, but a letter from the registrar or supervising faculty member, on college stationery, indicating that the applicant is a full-time student at college level or above must accompany the application.

If you join the ASMP, which requires a fee that is determined by your membership status, benefits are as follows:

1. Access to ASMP seminars and workshops.

2. Mutual support and access to other ASMP members.

3. You receive the ASMP Bulletin, a monthly publication for the professional photographer providing legal news, marketing informa-

tion, technical coverage, interviews, and discussions, essays, and news of other members.

4. Group Insurance Plans (the Major Medical plan, as stated above, is not available to Assistant Members).

5. ASMP Stock Picture Handbook that gives detailed information on stock agents throughout the world.

6. ASMP Professional Business Practices in Photography—a book that can help *any* photographer.

7. ASMP Books, a directory of ASMP members who specialize in advertising and stock photography, showing samples of their work, and a list of all ASMP members.

8. White Papers, which are exclusive reports covering special seminars.

9. Membership Directory, which lists all ASMP members alphabetically and geographically, including assignment and stock specialties, addresses, and phone numbers.

10. Press Card.

11. Group discounts on auto rentals.

12. Participation in exhibits, where members' work is chosen by merit and exhibited at the chapter or national level.

For more information about the ASMP, contact their national headquarters (see Appendix).

*Professional Photographers of America.* The PP of A is the oldest and largest association for professional photographers formed over 100 years ago. As an international association of 13,000 members and 200 affiliated organizations active in all facets of professional photography—though the bulk of membership seems to be photographers in the wedding and portrait category—the PP of A tries to offer members the ". . . tools, contacts, information and resources to help you advance and succeed," as a professional photographer.

The PP of A, like the ASMP, has a number of different categories for membership. They are as follows:

1. Portrait/Commercial (Professional Active)—an individual in the

business of photography and available for assignments, who conforms to applicable laws as they pertain to a business establishment, and has signed a Code of Ethics to be on file at PP of A headquarters.

2. Portrait/Commercial (Professional Additional Active)—available to employees of Active members only.

3. Industrial (Professional Active)—inplant photographer, or one who is employed in a photographic capacity within a company or other organization.

4. Industrial (Professional Additional Active)—available to employees of Active members only.

5. Photographic Educator (Professional Active)—full-time photography instructor at a state or province accredited college, university, technical institute, or school of photography.

6. International (Professional Active)—individual in professional photography residing outside the U.S. and Canada.

7. Sustaining—manufacturer or distributor of photographic equipment, laboratories, publishers, and firms providing services to photographers.

8. Service Specialist—an individual providing handcraft service to the photographic professional or employed as a lab technician, like a color artist or retoucher.

9. Retired—an individual who must have been a PP of A Professional member for at least five years immediately prior to application for this category.

10. Associate Professional—an individual engaged in a primary occupation other than photography, but is an occasional maker of photographs.

11. Colleague—an individual engaged in publication, marketing, management, research, professional services, or other fields of interest to professional photography. This classification is not for photographers.

12. Student—an individual preparing for a career in photography and enrolled on a full-time basis in an approved state or province accredited college. The student must submit proof of academic transcript.

The benefits of joining the PP of A are many and varied.

1. Access to annual convention, which includes a photographic trade show, educational seminars, and print displays. While open to the public, PPA members get a discount on admission.

2. Bank Card Service Program which provides a 2.22% studio service rate on Visa and MasterCard sales.

3. Business Forms which include studio contracts, wedding contracts, and a model release.

4. Access to a comprehensive study of photographic business operations which is available to PPA members at a discount.

5. Car Rental Discount.

6. Certified Professional Photographer and Certified Professional Photographic Specialist Programs to a national recognition, standards, and marketing program designed to demonstrate technical and artistic competence as well as business ethics through examination and critical review by PP of A members.

7. Consumer Redress Program, to assist the photographer and consumer when there's a disagreement, and direct satisfaction has not been achieved.

8. Degree Program—A professional identity program which recognizes achievement and service with the Master of Photography, Photographic Craftsman and Photographic Specialist degrees.

9. Equipment Insurance.

10. Group Insurance—which entitles members to a $1,000 free Accidental Death and Dismemberment and Disability Income (ugh!!). Group Major Medical, Term Life Insurance programs are offered at competitive rates.

For more information about PP of A benefits, as well as costs of membership—they're different for each category—contact the Professional Photographers of America (see Appendix).

## BUILDING NEW CONTACTS

If you're already getting jobs and networking contacts, you should think about building new contacts. The time to search for more work is when you're busy. That may seem like a contradiction, but it's not. What do you do *after* you go through an especially busy period, and hit a time span, of a week to a month or more, where you aren't getting any assignments? If you search for more work when you're busy, you'll rarely find yourself in this predicament. There's another point to consider, too.

When a person is "strapped for cash", like a period of forced inactivity, he wastes time worrying, which adversely affects his marketing. If you press the market while you're heavy with work however, you may be a little more tired, but you're not going to have to worry about where your next job is coming from. This is all-important, especially for a photographer who has a family to support.

To build new contacts, go back and revise Contact List B. Any sources of potential clients that have, in the interim, become clients, should be transferred to Contact List A. Then, begin contacting the people on Contact List B who didn't give you work the first time out, and add more names to the list of people who can possibly provide you with work.

Actually, a revision of your contact lists should be an ongoing process, but the best time to do it is when you're busy. It will seem like a chore, but it won't be a *necessity* for survival.

## THE REP

In order to spend the bulk of their time creating photography, many photographers elect to hire a rep.

Rep is actually slang for personal representative. The job of the photographer's personal representative is to go out and solicit work among prospective clients. How do they do that?

"I read *Ad Week*, *Graphic Design*, all the publications that talk about where the advertising accounts are going," says Lauren Morse. Lauren is the personal representative of Alan Zenreich, the talented special effects photographer.

"What I do is understand that Alan's photographic strengths are, and then go out and solicit the type of accounts that lend themselves to Alan's photographic style."

Lauren's solicitations can take a number of forms. She may make "cold" calls to art directors telling them about Alan's work, and his credits. If she can interest the art directors enough, Lauren will get an appointment to come into the advertising agency and show them Alan's portfolio. The process of communication is conducted in the same way the photographer would conduct it himself if he were there. But in this case, the photographer is back in the studio making money shooting.

After her initial appointment, Lauren will make follow-up calls to find out if Alan's got the job, or to just thank the art director for his time. She also makes sure to send a hand-written note saying how much of a pleasure it was meeting the art director. Why hand-written? Isn't it less professional than typing it out on letterhead? Lauren responds:

"A hand-written note always gets read. It shows a personal interest. I've found that people will open a personal letter faster than a business one.

"One thing I make sure is not to send anything to an art director in a plain white envelope. It won't get opened. I go for things that get attention, like writing the word "ART DIRECTOR" across the top of an envelope in bold, block letters."

*Promotions.* One thing a rep has the time to do that a photographer frequently doesn't is a promotion.

A promotion is *anything* that's designed to catch a potential client's interest without offending him.

"I did an interesting promotion involving a mailing tube," recalls Lauren. "What I did was to get a red mailing tube. I stenciled Alan's name on it in a type face used ordinarily to write TNT. Then I stuck a white pipe cleaner in one end to make it look like a fuse. Attached to the end of that was a piece of gold tinsel, which made the fuse look like it was lit. The effect was to make the red mailing tube look like a *live* stick of burning dynamite.

"Inside was the charge: a copy of Alan's page from *American Showcase* (a publication read by art directors where commercial photographers elect to advertise), with a computer graphic note that introduced Alan.

"This promotion cost money to produce. But it's paid for itself ten times over," Lauren concludes.

Another creative promotion that Alan and Lauren came up with jointly, involved the PBS television series, *A Hitchhiker's Guide To The Galaxy.* They had found out that art directors were great fans of the series, perhaps because of its dynamic graphics.

"That's when I got the idea to have a *Hitchhiker's* retrospective in our studio," Lauren says.

They decided to make this promotion fun. One night they'd invite friends and relatives, the next art directors and other people they either did business with or wanted to do business with.

All of the *Hitchhiker* episodes had been recorded on their VCR, so access wasn't a problem. Problem was, there were over seventy art directors and their friends on their list of invitees. They couldn't have all those people gathered around a TV set. To solve the problem Alan rented a projection TV, with a fifteen foot screen. They also had everyone bring their favorite food.

The retrospective was a resounding success. The art directors not only enjoyed themselves, some of them gave Alan business at a later date. So, the more creative your rep's promotions, the more work you will get.

## GETTING A REP

The first thing you're going to want is an established rep. Do not contract with a rep who isn't established.

I know one photographer who goes through reps like a fashion photographer exposing film. He's always getting some attractive young woman who projects a business-like demeanor to rep him in addition to her regular job. You know what usually happens?

This photographer's rep gets her client very few jobs. Because she's not a professional, she doesn't know the techniques of her trade. It's obvious to art directors and other clients of the photographer that she doesn't know what she's doing.

So, to protect your reputation, and your present clientele, only use a rep that is a member of the Society of Photographers' and Artists' Representatives, nicknamed SPAR. Their address is 514 East 83 Street, New York, NY 10028.

*Spar Reps.* "In order to become a member of SPAR, you have to have been repping for at least a year on your own," says Lauren Morse. "Then, before you become a full-fledged member, you have to take an orientation course that's divided into six sections that teaches you everything you need to know about repping, including how to handle the rejection that's inherent in the job.

"When the coursework is completed, you are then a member of SPAR."

As Lauren continued to explain to me, SPAR membership is important because it gives the rep a great degree of credibility. Until SPAR came along, reps were considered to be the dregs of the photographic industry. No one will say what percentage, but many reps before SPAR were poorly trained, and free to financially manipulate the photographer. But SPAR has made great strides in making the profession of photographer's personal representative legitimate, and in raising the standards for being a rep.

## THE CHOICE

Should you hire a rep? After all, they usually get 25% of the fee the photographer gets for an assignment, with an additional 5% for an assignment that involves traveling. That's a big chunk of your business.

Still, it pays to hire the rep if you're interested in expanding your business. You'll have to trust someone else for a change to go out and "pitch" your work. But, you won't have to go out and do it yourself. You'll be free to do what you do best—photograph.

## COPYRIGHT

The one consideration that photographers are always concerned about, once they get an assignment, is what rights do I sell to my photographs? In other words, once the photograph is made and sold, who retains copyright?

Under the most recent copyright law that went into effect on January 1, 1978, copyright stems from the moment of creation. So, as soon as you take a photograph, you and nobody else own the rights to it, all rights. Period.

But it isn't going to do you any good to own the copyright to a photograph that is just sitting around. You own the legal right to it and nothing else. In other words, you haven't made any money on the photograph. That comes when you sell it. Usually, a photographer will sell first rights to his photographs. This means that he is selling the first rights to publish his photograph to his client.

The idea is to maintain the copyright to your photographs. Essentially, when you sell first rights, you're selling a portion of the copyright for a limited amount of time, specifically the time when the photograph runs in a magazine, brochure, or some other format. In the case of wedding and portrait photographers, you're simply selling the rights to *one* print and nothing more. You retain the copyright.

By retaining the copyright to your photographs, you can sell them again. This is sometimes known as second rights. What this means is, you're selling a new client the rights to publish your photographs a second time. You've made it clear to the new client that he is the second person publishing your photographs.

Second rights are frequently sold to post card and greeting card publishers, as well as for stock. Stock photo houses essentially act as your agent in selling the second rights to your photographs to other interested parties, like magazines and newspapers.

In the case of stock photo agencies specifically, they will keep selling second rights to your photographs, *ad infinitum*, to any client who wants to purchase those rights.

Every time the photographer's picture is printed someplace, the photographer and the stock photo agency share the fee. Usually, this split is fifty/fifty.

Please note that you may also sell first rights and then second rights to photographs that are used for stock. It all depends whether they have been published before they wind up at the stock photo agency.

## WORK FOR HIRE

To a photographer, work for hire is the ugliest phrase in the English language. Quite simply, when you do a work for hire, it means you've sold *all* rights to your photographs. The copyright is no longer yours, but the client's, who can do with your photographs as he so chooses.

For obvious financial reasons, you should always try *not* to do a work for hire. I can think of two times where it might be necessary, though, to give in. One, when you're being paid so much for your photographs that it pays to sell them outright and two, when you absolutely need the money you're going to realize from a work for hire and can't wait to sell your photographs someplace else.

# CHAPTER TEN

# PERSONAL PUBLICITY AND PROMOTION

With your business firmly established, it's now time to consider getting free publicity. Publicity or public relations, as it's sometimes referred to, is a little understood concept because there's no accurate measure of the success of a publicity promotion. For instance, you appear on a television talk show (which can be very easy to get booked on) to publicize an exhibit of your photographs at a local gallery. Subsequently, gallery attendance increases. It's an unprovable hypothesis that gallery attendance increased as a direct result of your television appearance.

It could be that good weather prompted people to come to the exhibit, and that would account for the increased attendance. Perhaps the gallery took out a paid advertisement in a local newspaper publicizing the exhibit. Either could have increased attendance.

The point is, publicity is a means of generating interest, but there's no way of measuring the outcome. What publicity can do is create or increase a photographer's credibility among the public and your specific business relationships.

In the above situation where you're going on television, or even radio (which is a little more accessible), your clients might be impressed. Their confidence in your abilities is only heightened and supported by your public appearance. However, a magazine editor whom you've approached to do a layout or profile about you and your work, will not be so impressed.

The magazine people *are* the media. To them, television and radio are just other facets of the communications business. In fact, many magazine editors have already appeared on television or have been heard over the radio, as experts in their field. They are not easily impressed.

In essence, media exposure in magazines, newspapers, on television and radio, exists to impress current clients and gain future ones, all of which puts money in your pocket. Show an art director at an advertising agency a layout you recently got in *Popular Photography*, and they will be impressed. They know how many photographers compete for this type of exposure and respect the photographer who manages to break through the pack to be seen as an individual. This doesn't mean, of course, that a layout or a profile in a magazine will get you a job, but it certainly can't hurt. It can only help your business to prosper.

## LAYOUTS AND PROFILES

Photography magazines are divided into two basic types. The trade magazine is available to professional photographers by subscription only. The consumer photography magazine is sold on newstands and by subscription. Both types of magazine feature photographers in one of two contexts: a layout or a profile.

In a layout, the photographer's pictures appear, sometimes with captions, sometimes without. Basically, the images have to be strong enough to stand on their own without a lot of accompanying text.

A profile is a look, ". . . up close and personal," as ABC Sports might put it, of a photographer and his work. Usually what happens is a photography magazine editor will assign a freelance writer, such as myself, to interview and write a profile of a photographer they're interested in. My job is to interview the photographer, write an incisive profile (it helps if you are interviewing an interesting *person*), pick the photographs to accompany the article, then send it all in to the editor.

Sometimes the interest in a particular photographer stems from the editor. Sometimes it stems from the writer who has queried the editor about a photographer whose work he either admires or feels would be suitable for inclusion in the editor's magazine.

While a profile might at first glance seem a more prestigious way to present yourself, it's not necessarily a measure of a photographer's worth whether or not he gets a profile or a layout. What determines whether a photographer gets a layout or profile? It's simply the editorial requirements, and in some instances, the whim of the editor.

So if you find yourself in a situation where someone offers you a layout in their magazine, don't hold out for a profile because you're enamored with your own self-importance. For every photographer who gets a layout, there are thousands who do not get the opportunity, and the same holds true for a profile.

*An Editor's View.* Barry Tanenbaum is the editor of *Lens* and *Lens' On Campus* magazines. Frequently, he comes up with ideas for articles in interesting ways. For instance, a couple of years ago he was at a trade photography show and saw a startling picture of a fencer at the Hasselblad booth. He realized he wanted that picture on the cover of *Lens' On Campus*.

Tanenbaum then assigned me to track down the photographer, find out who he was, and see if he had more good images to flesh out an article. As it turned out, the photographer was Bob Kiss, who did have more pictures we could use. The result was an article about Kiss and his work in *Lens' On Campus*. And, on the cover of that issue was Kiss's photo—the one that Tanenbaum had admired at the photo trade show.

Other times, Tanenbaum gets ideas for layouts and profiles from regular contributors to his magazine who are freelance writers and photographers. He prefers to be contacted by mail if you have an idea for a story, or if you want to present your portfolio for possible inclusion in either of the magazines he edits. However, what he says he prefers most of all is "Money under the table." Tanenbaum has an interesting sense of humor.

*A Freelancer's View.* Many of the layouts and profiles, as Tanenbaum points out, are generated by freelance writers. Let me talk from my own personal experience and tell you what I look for in a photographer who I'm interested in working with.

First and foremost, his photographs have to be dynamite. Not flashy, not slick, but a combination of intelligence and technical competency. It's not as important that the photographer be a nice guy, but it certainly helps. Nothing's more boring than a person who think's he's god's gift to photography; I don't want to work with him, and I don't know any freelancer who, given a choice, would.

I can remember interviewing Burt Glinn, a man at the top of his profession. I was surprised and charmed by his humility, when so many photographers whom I'd previously interviewed with half his talent, went on about the "social significance" of their work. They weren't even photojournalists!

So, technical competence, intelligence, and humility are all important things to project. Also, the photographer, within reason, should be as free with his time as possible to answer the writer's questions, including follow-up questions while the article is being written.

The photographer should make his photographs and slides easily available for selection purposes, and should forward them without delay to the magazine once the writer has made his selection. The really smart photographers will have a duped set of slides and photographs that the writer may take with him at the time of the initial interview and/or viewing of his images.

## SOME ADVICE

When trying to decide which magazines to approach, use this criteria:

- Which magazine will give me a better looking layout?
- Which magazine pays for photos and which doesn't?
- Do they pay on acceptance or on publication?

Remember that editors need product. They always like to look at good stuff. And, remember that you should be honest and straight with an editor. If you've already submitted work to another magazine, let him know that. Don't promise an editor an exclusive which you know for a fact you can't deliver. You have your reputation to consider, and it will follow you wherever you go.

## EDITORIAL CONTACTS

Freelancers can be contacted by writing to them care of the magazine that they usually write for. If you wish to contact the photography magazines directly, in general you'll find that the consumer photography magazines have more editorial stability. This is because those jobs are more prestigious and harder to come by than their trade counterparts, and they pay more, too.

*Consumer Magazines.* The magazines listed below are the consumer magazines I would go after to either publish my work or do a layout of my photographs. Although there are others, I feel that these will do your business the most good.

1. *POPULAR PHOTOGRAPHY*, 1 Park Avenue, New York, New York 10016
*Popular Photography* is designed for advanced amateurs and professional photographers. It concerns itself mainly with instructional articles, like how a photographer approached a particularly challenging problem, reviews of new equipment and film emulsions, as well as layouts and profiles of professional photographers. Selection of cover photographs is the responsibility of Monica Cipnic, Picture Editor. Arthur Goldsmith, the Editorial Director, has the final say on which photographers are profiled. He works in consultation with his editors who may forward ideas for profile and layouts of photographers. Steve Pollock, the Features Editor, is a good person to initially contact if you want this magazine to give you some coverage.

2. *AMERICAN PHOTOGRAPHER*, 1515 Broadway, New York, New York 10036
This is more of a mainstream publication that appeals not only to those with an advanced understanding of photography, but those who want to find out what's happening in the broadest areas of photography. With technical features minimized, much of its editorial content is profiles and layouts of professional photographers. It's a very difficult magazine to break into, but any coverage in it carries a lot of prestige. Contact Sean Callahan, the Editor, for further particulars.

3. *MODERN PHOTOGRAPHY*, 825 Seventh Ave., New York, New York 10019
Most of the material in this magazine is generated by staffers, and little of it is written freelance. The editorial content tends toward the technical. But, if you have some interesting idea for an article about your work, try contacting the magazine's publisher, Bert Keppler.

4. *PETERSEN'S PHOTOGRAPHIC MAGAZINE*, 8490 Sunset Blvd., Los Angeles, California 90069
Petersen's emphasizes how-to photography articles, with an occasional interview with a photographer, including publishing some of his pictures. Contact the publisher, Paul R. Farber, for more information.

*Trade Magazines.* There are six trade photography magazines that also do profiles and occasional layouts of professional photographer's work.

1. *THE RANGEFINDER*, 1312 Lincoln Blvd., Santa Monica, California 90406
*The Rangefinder* concentrates heavily on how-to articles for the pro "shooter," and also includes in its editorial package, business articles, profiles, and layouts of professional photographers who work in a variety of categories. The magazine's art direction is quite good, and so is the reproductive quality, especially when compared to other trade magazines. Contact editor Arthur Stern or publisher Steve Sheanin.

2. *PHOTO DISTRICT NEWS*, 167 Third Avenue, New York, New York 10003
*Photo District News* is thought of among professional photographers as the finest magazine at addressing their *business* needs. The magazine, which is set up in tabloid format, gives the reader a lot of insight into what it's like to be a pro. While many of the articles deal with business related topics, there are occasional technical tips from pros, and some profiles. Contact Carl Pugh, the publisher, if you want to get involved with *Photo District News*.

3. *PHOTOGRAPHER'S FORUM*, 25 W. Anapamu, Santa Barbara, California 93101
This is a magazine that appeals to photography students as well as photographers. It features profiles and layouts of professional photographers. The reproduction of photographs is excellent, and so is the layout. Because this publication is not as mainstream as the others, competition to get in is not as intense. If you want to be published here, contact Glen Serbin, the magazine's editor-in-chief.

4. *STUDIO PHOTOGRAPHY*, PTN Publishing, 101 Crossways Park West, Woodbury, New York 11797.
Since I was once the editor of this magazine, I have an intimate knowledge of its editorial content. In my opinion, some of the articles offer practical equipment and how-to tips for the wedding and portrait photographer only. If you wind up getting a layout or a profile of you and your work in this magazine, it could be used as part of a direct mail promotion—especially for wedding and portrait photographers.

5. *THE PROFESSIONAL PHOTOGRAPHER*, 1090 Executive Way, Des Plaines, Illinois 60018.
This magazine is published by the Professional Photographers of America. Its basic appeal is to wedding and portrait photographers. Articles contain information on how to build your business, and how to take better pictures. Layouts of photographer's photographs are included in the latter type of story. Because the art direction and the quality of the printing is quite good, especially for the wedding and portrait photographer, this is a wonderful place to develop portfolio material. Contact editor Gordon Biberle for more information.

6. *PHOTOMETHODS*, 1 Park Avenue, New York, New York 10016
*Photomethods* appeals to more technically-oriented photographers. The editorial package includes how-to stories that will help the reader in his work; personal experiences of photographers that will also help benefit the reader; and a rare photo feature on a photographer and his work. Editor Fred Schmidt can provide you with more information.

*Two Other Magazines.* There are two other photography magazines whose distribution puts them in a class by themselves. They are the previously mentioned *Lens* and *Lens' On Campus.*

*Lens* is purchased directly by camera dealers and given to their customers in camera stores. The magazine is designed to promote and build business for the dealer. But the reader also benefits, too, because *Lens* has darkroom and equipment tips, as well as profiles of photographers. It's distributed nationwide and relies heavily on professional photographers for its editorial content.

*Lens' On Campus* is distributed free of charge to students enrolled in photo courses at universities and colleges around the country. It contains profiles, portfolios and interviews with professional photographers.

The address for both magazines is 645 Stewart Avenue, Garden City, New York 11550.

## PAYMENT

The trade photography magazines do not pay for the photographer's work; the consumer photography magazines do. However, this does not mean you should eliminate querying trade magazines. When you're first starting out, any publicity, whether you get paid for your photographs or not, is good publicity.

In fact, you should always look at publicity not for the immediate benefit, but for what it will do for your career in the long run. As I said earlier, the purpose of publicity is to get your name and your work before the picture buyers. You may receive response from an article about your work months after that article has appeared.

As a good business person, you should keep the cash flow in mind. Begin by contacting the consumer publications (but remember that in some instances you will not be paid until your work is published). At the same time, don't discount the trades, as their publicity may bring you assignments worth far more than any magazine could pay for a profile piece.

## CHAPTER ELEVEN

# GETTING PUBLICITY IN OTHER MEDIA

Another type of publicity a photographer can try for involves developing a business relationship with a camera company. The idea behind this type of publicity is to get the camera company to promote *you.* I can think of no better example than that of Walter Iooss, Jr.

### PRODUCT ENDORSEMENTS

Iooss is one of the country's best sports photographers, who for many years has been a mainstay at *Sports Illustrated.* Still, to the general public, he was unknown, until 1984.

In 1984, Iooss began appearing on nationally televised and local talk shows. If you were watching, you would have seen him come out and speak about his then current project, called "Shooting For The Gold." He had been employed by Fuji Film to shoot American's Olympic athletes in training. He was flying all over the world, from international athletic meets like the Pan Am Games to the Olympic training facility in Colorado Springs, to shoot the athletes.

Iooss had signed a business agreement with Fuji Film to do "Shooting For The Gold" and in the process promote Fuji Film. It was a brilliant idea. Take a crackerjack photographer, send him around-the-world to shoot the athletes in an historical time when patriotism was running high, and then promote his work in the visual media.

Iooss's photographs were subsequently exhibited at museums in many American cities, and in United Airlines terminals. Prior to the beginning of the Olympics, a select group of his photos were auctioned off to benefit the various amateur athletic foundations. The auction received local publicity in Los Angeles where it took place. The project was also mentioned in articles in national magazines.

After the Olympics, a book of Iooss's photos with text by *New York Times* sports columnist Dave Anderson, was published under the name "Shooting For The Gold."

In addition to the fee Iooss got for the project, he received incalculable amounts of free publicity, as a result of all the promotion done by Fuji's public relations agency, Daniel J. Edelman.

The architect of the "Shooting For The Gold" promotion was Edelman account supervisor David Reid Fox. Reflecting on his publicity efforts, Fox says:

"The primary value of any photographer going on TV to promote his work is the recognition factor. People come to know his name and reputation. But a careful line has to be drawn between a photographer who goes on TV to promote himself, or to promote a product.

"I think that a sheer product endorsement has some effect on the consumer. There's a backlash to it. People aren't stupid. They know when someone is being paid to say something. It's only when a photographer believes in a product and he has something to show for it, like Walter's photos which were all shot on Fuji Film, that the photographer has any credibility. Then you have a simultaneous promotion of the product and the photographer's work, his photography. Everyone wins from this situation."

How then can a professional photographer develop a business relationship with a company that's designed to promote the photographer's name and reputation, which can lead to more jobs?

"I would suggest," Fox continues, "for the photographer to do a little ground work before contacting the public relations arm of a camera company or film manufacturer, the entities that make the initial decisions before approaching their client for final approval on a project.

"Don't rely on the public relations agency to come up with the idea for a promotion. The photographer should do his homework, do some research, and come up with an idea to promote a company's product, using himself, the photographer, as a promotional tool. Then he should contact the public relations agency that represents the particular product he wants to promote and hit them with a detailed, written proposal.

"Once you submit the proposal, you can then do your follow up. But no one will see you on a cold appointment basis, if they don't have that proposal in their hands to begin with. And make sure that the proposal contains marketing and merchandising information."

In 1983, I began receiving public relations releases about Walter Iooss, Jr's., project with Fuji Film. The releases continued over the next year. Finally, in 1984, I was convinced of the scope and national interest of Iooss's photographs.

I contacted Ted Kreiter, the executive editor of *The Saturday Evening Post* and Pat Perry, the associate editor who deals with all assignments involving photographers I've already mentioned. After they held a meeting, I was assigned to do an article about Iooss and his project. This is how a public relations promotion eventually winds up as an article in a national magazine.

Who profits from such an article?

The photographer, who gets a whole bunch of free publicity.

The "client," Fuji Film, whose product is briefly mentioned.

The reader, who gets to see some unusually good and special photographs, and read an interesting story that contains details of what were, at the time, Olympic hopefuls.

The writer who gets paid by the magazine to write the article about the photographer.

SHOOTING FOR THE GOLD

CONTACT: DANIEL J. EDELMAN, INC.
In Los Angeles: Michelle Lawrence
213/553-1560
In New York: Paul Drexel
212/757-9100

FUJI PHOTO FILM U.S.A., INC.
In New York: Thomas H. Shay
212/736-3335

WALTER IOOSS, JR.

"SHOOTING FOR THE GOLD" PHOTOGRAPHER

Walter Iooss, Jr. is one of the world's most renowned professional sports photographers. He has been associated with Sports Illustrated for more than 20 years, having almost 200 covers to his credit.

Iooss literally grew up at Sports Illustrated. A native of East Orange, NJ, he began his career at the magazine as a freelance photographer; his first picture was published when he was only 16. In the past 23 years, Iooss' work has also appeared in such publications as Time, Newsweek, Esquire, Playboy, People, Fortune, Natural History and Money, as well as in numerous books covering sports.

In June 1982, Iooss left his position as Senior Staff Photographer at Sports Illustrated to pursue what he calls the "assignment of a lifetime" -- producing "Shooting For The Gold," a dramatic photodocumentary that traces the arduous journey of American athletes to the 1984 Los Angeles Olympic Games. Iooss has traveled across the United States to training sites and competitions to photograph the incredible spirit and determination of America's athletes as they reach for an Olympic Gold Medal.

This unprecedented assignment has been underwritten by Fuji Photo Film U.S.A., Inc., an Official Sponsor of the 1984 U.S. Olympic Team and the Official Film of the Los Angeles 1984 Olympics.

*This was the first release Fuji sent out, briefly explaining the project they had commissioned Iooss to do.*

In his long career as a sports photographer, Iooss has covered many Olympic Games, including the 1976 Olympics in Montreal. His incredible photographs of decathlete Bruce Jenner's Gold Medal-winning triumph captured one of the most memorable moments in sports history.

Iooss considers "Shooting For The Gold" to be one of his most difficult and demanding assignments to date. In 1983, Iooss covered the Pan-American Games in Caracas, Venezuela for the project. He exposed more than 200 rolls of Fuji film in 12 days, photographing 23 different sports.

"The Olympic Games in Los Angeles are guaranteed to be one of the biggest sports events of all time," says Iooss. "To photograph America's finest athletes in more than 20 competition sports, I'll have to shoot hundreds of rolls of film while trying to find that different photograph. I want to show the emotion of the athletes, the spirit that drives them to train for years to compete in an event that can be over in split-seconds. And at the same time, I want to photograph all the sports. I want to show gymnastics and judo, and swimming and shooting as these events have never been portrayed before.

"The Pan-American Games gave me a taste of what to expect in Los Angeles in July," continues Iooss. "In order to photograph so many different sports in several locations, all with different lighting, I had to plan a very tight schedule, but then leave room for last minute changes. At the same time, I continued to search for that special photograph, on the sidelines, in the eyes, gestures or postures of the athletes. The photographs in 'Shooting For The Gold' are meant to have a special quality that communicates the very heart of competition. It truly is the assignment of a lifetime. I've been granted creative freedom and an unprecedented time frame rarely offered to sports photographers."

Iooss has garnered many honors and awards for his photographs, including the title of NFL Photographer of the Year in 1979. His work has been exhibited at the International Center of Photography in New York City, Photokina in Europe, and as part of "Man in Sport," an internationally traveled exhibit.

## PUBLIC RELATIONS

If you come up with a proposal that involves a camera or film company's product, direct it, as Fox suggested, to the company's public relations representative. If you direct your proposal to the company first, they will just kick it down to the agency for their opinion anyway before taking any final action.

Here is a brief list of some of the public relations agency's that field and sometimes act upon proposals from professional photographers. Depending on how good a businessperson you are, you can get a very nice fee for becoming what is, in essence, a product spokesperson.

I suggest, however, that for The Rowland Company as well as all the other companies in this list, do your initial contact by mail as David Reid Fox suggested. Then do a follow up phone call. I have also included in the list the name of the account executive or account supervisor at the public relations agency who fields the proposals from professional photographers.

1. The Rowland Company, 415 Madison Avenue, New York, New York 10017
The Rowland Company represents Canon, USA. The gentleman to contact there is account supervisor Lyman Gaylord. Canon works with professional photographers on a continual basis, usually through Canon Professional Service. For instance, fine art photographer Jacques Kaplan uses Canon equipment, and Canon has helped promote Kaplan's gallery exhibits by arranging television and magazine publicity.

Canon also sponsors the Pictures of the Year contest. Since the Canon name is prominently displayed on much of the press materials, Canon indirectly receives publicity. As we were "going to press," I found out that Canon will be sponsoring a *college* version of the Pictures of the Year contest. Judges will be current Pictures of the Year winners. Prizes awarded to the winning college students will include apprenticeships at various publications around the country.

2. Strear, David & Mitchell, Inc., 575 Madison Avenue, Suite 1006, New York, New York 10022
Nikon, Inc. employs this firm as their public relations representatives.

Nikon has worked with many photographers in the past, usually providing them with free equipment and the use of their public relations apparatus, in return for the photographer giving Nikon a story about how they used their equipment.

Some of the Nikon promotions have involved photographers who weren't all that well-known. For instance, they gave equipment to Roni Neuer and Herb Libertson, New York City art gallery owners who mounted an expedition that found a lost tribe in Indonesian New Guinea. Not only did they get camera equipment to take pictures, they had an exhibition of their pictures at New York's Nikon House, a photo gallery that Nikon runs. There was a lot of attendant publicity surrounding the gallery opening and Neuer and Libertson's discovery.

In addition to deciding on which proposals his clients should act upon, Strear also has a large amount of input into the selection of photographer's work for exhibition at Nikon House. Even for the most mundane shows, Nikon will inform the photographic and general media about the time of the show and the show's content.

3. Bozell and Jacobs, 6 East 43 St., New York, New York 10017
Bozell and Jacobs represents Minolta, and the contact there is Rick Sammon, an agency vice-president. Bozell and Jacobs has been heavily involved in recent years with photographers who help to promote their products. Photographers they have worked with include Harry Benson and Robert Farber. They seem to be very open about considering proposals, but my impression is that the proposal must be solidly in Minolta's interest before they will commit to it.

4. Olympus Camera Corp, Crossways Park West, Woodbury, New York 11797
Olympus maintains an in-house public relations department, and the contact there is Jess Wilkes. Out of the four major camera companies mentioned, Olympus seems to work the least with professional photographers. This may be changing, though. They have a committment to place their products squarely in front of pro "shooters" with whom they would like to work. So, my advice is to contact Olympus first because they are in the position of playing "catch up" ball and may be very interested in a proposal that helps them do that.

CANON USA, INC., ONE CANON PLAZA, LAKE SUCCESS, NEW YORK 11042

**NEWS FROM Canon®**

RELEASE DATE: IMMEDIATE

CONTACT: Mike Matzkin (516) 588-6700
Lyman Gaylord (The Rowland Co.) (212) 688-1200

CANON ANNOUNCES PHOTO ESSAYIST AWARD

Major Part of Pictures of the Year Contest

LAKE SUCCESS, N.Y., Sept. 20 -- Canon U.S.A., Inc. today announced that its award in the prestigious University of Missouri/ National Press Photographers Association Pictures of the Year competition (POY) will honor outstanding photo essayists.

"There are no subject matter requirements or limits for the Canon Photo Essayist competition," said Fujio Mitarai, president of Canon U.S.A., Inc. "The images can have been made over any time period and they need not have been published," he continued.

Entries will be judged solely on the basis of how thoughtfully and skillfully the photographer examined his or her subject matter and how clearly the theme or storyline is presented, Mr. Mitarai said. "The photo essay is one of the most challenging assignments for the photojournalist and we are proud to be able to honor outstanding achievements in this area," he stated.

Canon is a sponsor of POY along with the University and NPPA and is funding it through an educational grant on a long term basis.

-more-

The Official 35mm Camera of the 1984 Olympic Games

Contributor to the U.S. Olympic Team

*These press releases show how Canon received publicity for the Pictures of the Year competition. Notice how Mary Ellen Mark, winner of Canon's Photo Essayist Award, is prominently mentioned.*

- 2 -

The company has commissioned creation of a piece of sculpture symbolic of the award. It, a Canon professional 35mm camera and $1,000 will be presented to the winning photo essayist at yearly ceremonies held in April at the University of Missouri. At the same time, Canon cameras and $1,000 each also go to the Newspaper Photographer of the Year and to the Magazine Photographer of the Year. Entrants in these categories submit portfolios of images that must have been made within the calendar year.

Entries will be judged in February, 1984 with the winners announced in March. Entry forms will be mailed to NPPA members in early October, 1983. Non-members may obtain entry forms by writing: Pictures of the Year Contest, Ken Kobre, Director, University of Missouri School of Journalism, Columbia, Mo. 65211, or National Press Photographers' Association, P.O. Box 1146, Durham, N.C. 27702.

# # #

From: The Rowland Company, Inc.
415 Madison Avenue
New York, N.Y. 10017
Lyman Gaylord
(212) 688-1200

For: POY

TOP WINNERS IN PICTURES OF
THE YEAR COMPETITION ARE NAMED

COLUMBIA, Mo., Feb. 20 -- The winners of the three most prestigious awards in the 41st Pictures of the Year competition were announced here today by POY contest director Ken Kobre.

The top winners are: Steve Ringman of the San Francisco Chronicle, Newspaper Photographer of the Year; James Nachtwey of Black Star, Magazine Photographer of the Year and Mary Ellen Mark of Archive Pictures, the winner of the new Canon Photo Essayist Award.

Pictures of the Year is sponsored by the National Press Photographers Association and the University of Missouri School of Journalism under an educational grant from Canon U.S.A., Inc.

Newspaper and Magazine Photographer of the Year entrants submitted portfolios of photos taken in 1983. Canon Photo Essayist Award entrants submitted stories shot over any time period.

All but one of the photos in Nachtwey's winning portfolio

(more)

-2-

were shot while he was on assignment for Time. Canon Award winner Mark did her essay on assignment for Life. All of Ringman's pictures were taken for the Chronicle.

Judges for the competition were Elisabeth Biondi, photo editor of GEO, Joseph Costa, professor of photojournalism at Ball State University, Muncie, Ind., Bruce Dale of the National Geographic, Jay Dickman, photographer for the Dallas Times-Herald, and Jim Richardson, a Denver Post staff photographer.

Twenty seven individual category winners will be announced shortly.

This year's Pictures of the Year competition attracted over 15,000 photos from more than 1,500 photographers.

Pictures of the Year awards will be formally presented on April 14 at the University of Missouri - Columbia at the start of Journalism Week. This year's Journalism Week, the 54th annual, will celebrate the Journalism School's diamond jubilee. It is the oldest school of Journalism in the U.S.

# # #

CONTACT: FRED ROSEN
Public Relations Department
Gilbert, Felix & Sharf
405 Lexington Avenue
(212) 867-8111

NEWS FROM

**Nikon house**

620 FIFTH AVENUE at ROCKEFELLER CENTER
NEW YORK, N.Y. 10020 • (212) 586-3907

JAN COBB'S "FREE DRINKS AND MAD SCHEMES",

AND PAMELA RANKIN-SMITH'S "REAR VIEWS",

BRIGHTEN THE SPRING AT NIKON HOUSE

NEW YORK -- Nikon House has emerged unscathed from the depth of Winter to brighten the New York Spring with the exhibit of Jan Cobb's eclectic "Free Drinks and Mad Schemes," and Pamela Rankin-Smith's perceptive "Rear Views."

Jan Cobb is one of the most respected and well-known names in the highly competitive field of commercial photography. In his exhibit in the downstairs Gallery at Nikon House, it's easy to see why. His unique and intelligent use of color as a graphic tool, coupled with his innate understanding of line, depth and form, produce photographs that transcend the commercial genre and step into the realm of art. At whatever part of a Jan Cobb photograph you look at, there's always something happening. His show in the Gallery includes nudes that are erotic and artistic at the same time and portraits where color and shadow mold his subjects in brassy, classy and sometimes surrealistic settings.

Pamela Rankin-Smith has come a long way, both geographically and aesthically, from her birthplace, the Lower Rio Grande

*This is a typical Nikon House release. Because the photographer is helping to promote the client, Nikon House, a news release about his gallery show is disseminated to local and national media.*

of Texas. She has become in her own words, "a full fledged New Yorker," whose black and white photographs are full of stark contrasts and emotion. The theme of her show in the upstairs Showcase, "Rear View," is an amusing look at people's derrieres. One of her primary subjects is her young granddaughter, photographed at her son's farm in Woodstock, New York.

Both shows will run from April 28 to May 17. Nikon House is located at 620 Fifth Avenue, on the Promenade at Rockefeller Center. Open Tuesday through Saturday, from 10AM to 5:45 PM, there is no charge for admission, making Nikon House the most educational, entertaining and economical attraction in New York this Spring.

# # #

**Bozell & Jacobs Public Relations**

A Division of Bozell & Jacobs, Inc., 6 East 43rd Street, New York, New York 10017 Phone: 212/916-8500

FOR IMMEDIATE RELEASE

CONTACT: Barbara Swab
Bozell & Jacobs Public Relations
6 East 43rd Street
New York, NY 10017
(212) 916-8500

or Robin Smithers
Wolf Camera And Video
150 14th Street Northwest
Atlanta, GA 30318
(404) 892-1707

FASHION PHOTOGRAPHER ROBERT FARBER

TO APPEAR AT WOLF CAMERA AND VIDEO'S ANNUAL FALL EXPO

Atlanta, Ga. -- Renowned fashion and fine art photographer Robert Farber will appear at Wolf Camera and Video's annual fall expo here, Friday and Saturday, November 2 and 3.

Farber, who uses Minolta equipment exclusively, will be at the Minolta booth to sign autographs and to offer photographic tips and technical information on the company's full line of products on Friday, November 2.

On Saturday, November 3, he will offer two lecture/slide shows -- one at 11:00 p.m.; the other at 4:00 p.m. The presentations are designed for photographers who are interested in fashion and fine art photography. Farber will emphasize the importance of form, tonality, shapes and lighting.

He will also offer tips on the following subjects:

- Career opportunities in fashion, fine art and commercial photography;
- Choosing the right equipment;
- Developing a fashion portfolio;
- How to build professional relationships with editors, agents and models;
- How fashion photography evolved into a serious art form and a multimillion dollar business.

*One of the most successful promotions mounted in the last few years by Minolta, was the selling of photographer Robert Farber. A fashion photographer, who's written extensively on the subject (Amphoto publishing), Farber uses Minolta equipment, a fact that Minolta has capitalized on.*

A self-taught photographer, Farber specializes in fashion, nude and fine art photography. His work has appeared in *Esquire*, *GQ*, *Vogue*, *Ladies Home Journal*, *Playboy* and *Penthouse*. His subjects have been some of the most famous models of today -- including Apollonia, Christie Brinkley, Jeri Hall, Patti Hanson, Rachel Ward and Beverly Johnson. Farber's commercial credits run from ads for Revlon and Paco Rabanne to movie posters for Paramount and Columbia.

He is also the author of five books, including *Professional Fashion Photography*, a widely received look at the inner working of the world of fashion. Farber's fifth book, *Farber Nudes*, was published last fall. He is currently working on a book initiated by Doubleday editor, Jacqueline Onassis. Entitled *By The Sea*, it is a collection of seascapes from around the world.

In addition, Farber's photographs are sold nationwide in the form of posters, greeting cards and limited edition gallery prints. He is also the subject of an entertaining videotape on fashion photography and has made numerous television appearances.

A selection of Farber's books and posters will be on sale at Wolf Camera and Video during the expo.

The show will be held Thursday, Friday, Saturday and Sunday, November 1, 2, 3 and 4. More than 50 manufacturers will be represented with continuous factory demonstrations throughout the show. There will be other celebrities, door prizes, auctions and use of a professional lighting system to photograph beautiful models at no charge.

The expo will take place at Wolf's main showroom at 150 14th Street N.W. Hours are: Thursday and Friday, November 1 and 2, 8:30 a.m. to 9:00 p.m.; Saturday, November 3, 9:00 a.m. to 7:00 p.m.; and Sunday, November 4, 12 noon to 6:00 p.m. Admission is free.

## DOING IT ON YOUR OWN

After contacting all the camera companies with your proposal, you've received polite brush-offs. It may happen; it may not. If it does, what do you do? Do you abandon the idea of getting free publicity? Of course not! There are other alternatives.

The nice thing is if you've got a phone, a pencil, paper, and some resource materials, you're in business. The only thing you may have trouble selecting is the resource materials.

There are publications, besides *Writer's Market* (see Appendix) which I mentioned earlier, that list newspapers, magazines and television and radio shows that might be interested in interviewing you. The first step is either to buy the reading material, or, to save money, borrow them from your local library. The second step is to carefully analyze each listing.

The idea is to query a potential source that interviews people like you. For instance, a television show that, according to a listing, is looking for experts in the health area, won't be interested in a photographer. But a show that deals with the arts, or as a policy, uses guests from a number of different backgrounds, would be worth querying.

## MEDIA OUTLETS

1. Radio Contacts, Larimi Communications Associates, Ltd., 151 East 50 St., New York, New York 10022
Published every year, *Radio Contacts* lists the names, addresses, telephone numbers, and staff of major market United States radio stations, networks, news services, and program producers. It contains complete descriptions of local, syndicated, and network interview programs including information and guest requirements. Of special interest is information on the number and length of news programs, information on regularly scheduled special features, the appropriate contacts in the news departments, target audiences, and the format for each station. If you buy the book, you will receive the Monthly Change Bulletins on significant new programs, personnel changes, and program updates, and Edit/Search. Edit/Search is a phone-in service to *Radio Contacts* research department for inquiries about program changes in major markets, like New York, Chicago, or Los Angeles.

2. TV Contacts, Larimi Communications Associates Ltd., 151 East 50 St., New York, New York 10022

*TV Contacts* contains the same information as its companion volume, except television rather than radio stations and programs are covered.

3. Bacon's Publicity Checker, Newspapers Vol. II, Bacon's Illinois Publishing Company, Inc. 332 Michigan Avenue, Chicago, Illinois 60604

Bacon's Publicity Checker, Newspapers, Vol. II, is a comprehensive directory and placement guide to the nation's daily and weekly newspapers. It is divided into three sections: Section I—the daily newspapers in the United States and Canada; Section II—the weekly and semi-weekly newspapers in the United States; Section III—the news services and syndicates, the Black press, and computer generated lists of newspapers which will give the user increased penetration for news releases and stories directed to the nation's major news outlets.

Also consider contacting the Superstations, those TV stations that sell their signal to cable services around the country and essentially act as syndicators. WGN-Chicago, WOR-TV New York, and WTBS-Atlanta (owned by Ted Turner) are all Superstations. If you appear on any interview program that either of these three local stations broadcast, you will be seen in thousands more homes around the country. These homes are subscribing to a basic cable service that contains the Superstation package. It's the closest thing to getting on a nationally televised talk show with half the effort.

## THE PITCH

Regardless of the media outlet that is going to be contacted, you're still going to have to pitch them over the phone, and then follow up with a letter or a news release (see accompanying illustrations).

The pitch can be drawn from the proposal you've already written for the public relations agency, but with the endorsement of a camera company's product eliminated. Since the camera company is not helping you, you're under no obligation to publicize them or their product.

What you are publicizing is you and your work. The work may be a gallery exhibit, an edition of limited prints you're selling, unusual photographs of exotic places, anything that visually and tangibly sets you apart from other photographers.

When speaking to the contact over the phone, be polite but confident. If *you* aren't convinced that you should be on the radio or television show, or have a newspaper do an article about you and your

November 1, 1984

---------------
---------------
---------------
---------------
---------------

Dear -----------:

On April 14, 1982, photojournalist Harry Benson was named "Magazine Photographer of the Year" by the University of Missouri School of Journalism and the National Press Photographers Association. The following year he was named runner-up in the same category and first prize winner in the portrait category. It is highly unusual for a photographer to be recognized two years in a row in this prestigious contest.

Harry has also been the recipient of numerous other awards including citations from the Overseas Press Club. In a career spanning 30 years, he has photographed some of the most famous personalities of our time -- the Beatles, Muhammed Ali, Halston, Brooke Shields, Grace Kelly, Greta Garbo, Michael Jackson, Clint Eastwood, Sophia Loren, the Kennedys, Carters, Nixons, Fords and Reagans, to name a few. His images have dominated spreads and covers for Life, People, New York magazine, French Vogue, Fortune, and many others.

Life magazine's November 1984 cover story features Harry's photographs of the 23 surviving children of former Presidents -- from Helen Taft Manning, 93, to Amy Carter, 17. A set of these photographs is being presented to the Smithsonian Institution's National Portrait Gallery.

I believe Harry would be an interesting interview subject for your (readers, viewers, listeners). He will be in Boston the week of November 26. A major exhibit of more than 160 of his photographs is currently "traveling" the country. It has been displayed at the Soho International Art Center, New York City, at the Southwest Craft Center in San Antonio, Texas, at the Art Center College of Design in Pasadena, at the Tucson Museum of Art, Tucson, Arizona and at Brooks Institute, Santa Barbara, California, to name a few. Another exhibit of his work will open at Harvard University this month.

*Here is an example of a typical "pitch" letter that a public relations agency sends out to the media, as they try to get publicity for a photographer that they are working with.*

Page 2

Other reasons why I think Harry would make an ideal guest on your show include:

- In the spring of 1982, Harmony Books published Harry's first book, Harry Benson on Photojournalism, featuring outstanding photographs and reminiscences of his photo assignments through the years.

- He has received numerous awards for his photo essays for Life and other magazines. These include: Robert Kennedy's assassination, President Nixon's resignation, the IRA hunger strikers of Northern Ireland, Alexander Solzhenitsyn, the starving children of Somalia and the Shock Trauma Unit at the University of Maryland.

Harry would be prepared to discuss each of the above topics and his exciting career in general. He is comfortable on television and very candid about his various assignments. I am enclosing additional background information for your review.

I will be in touch shortly to see if you are interested in interviewing him. In the meantime, should you have any questions about Harry's career, or if you would like to review other samples from his portfolio, please do not hesitate to call. My direct line number is (212) 916-8513.

Sincerely,

Barbara Swab
Vice President

BS/amm

Enclosure

work, then how do you expect to convince the contact on the other end of the phone line?

Be prepared to make a number of phone calls before you get to the person who can actually make a decision about whether you'll be interviewed or not. If the contact shows interest, that's the time to either send the letter or a news release that summarizes your pitch.

Look at the sample "pitch" letter. Notice how the photographer's credentials and honors are immediately mentioned, followed up by a brief list of some of the magazines where his work has appeared.

The writer then goes into an in-depth "pitch" as to why the photographer would be a good interview subject. The letter closes with an offer to the prospective "hit" to see the photographer's portfolio if they have any doubts, which they might, as to whether the photographer's work fits into their editorial format.

If you do your own "pitch" letters, this is a good, convincing format to follow. It sure worked for Minolta, considering the amount of publicity they got the photographer mentioned in the release.

## THE INTERVIEW

Newspaper reporters ask their own questions, but sometimes radio and television interviewers do not. They have staffers who write the questions and on some shows, the guest is asked by the producer or segment coordinator to come to the studio with his own list of questions. This happened to me on a television talk show.

The host had personally asked me before the taping to give him questions to ask me, which I did. When we taped, he went to his prepared list of questions, and I think he appreciated my assistance.

## PAID PROMOTION

If you've got the money, you can also pay for your promotion in the form of paid advertising.

An ad in the Yellow Pages can bring results, or for that matter, an ad in your local paper. But three publications distributed on a national level in which many commercial photographers elect to advertise are *American Showcase*, *Corporate Showcase*, and the *Creative Black Book*.

"*American Showcase* has been in business for nine years," *American Showcase* and *Corporate Showcase* spokesperson Julie Morris told me. "American Showcase, for commercial photographers, is a directory aimed at the general advertising industry.

"We're currently putting together the 4th edition of our *Corporate Showcase*. It's for photographers who do corporate work. It's aimed at organizations, like public relations agencies, ad agencies, and corporations that have need of corporate photographers."

A page in either of these directories will include a layout of the photographer's photographs with his name, address, and phone number. For more information on rates for either *Corporate* or *American Showcase*, contact Julie Morris at American Showcase Inc. (see Appendix).

The *Creative Black Book* lists services available to the advertising industry, including photography. Photographers may purchase one or more pages of advertising which would include a layout of their photographs plus the photographer's name, address, and phone number. For further information on pricing and services contact the *Creative Black Book* (see Appendix).

# Afterword
# HARRY M. WALKER

If it wasn't for Soapy Smith, Harry M. Walker might never have come to Skagway.

Skagway, Alaska, a coastal city, was a boom town in the 1890's, the entrance to the rich gold fields of the Yukon Territory. Soapy was an outlaw from the Old West, who'd come to Skagway to make money and terrorize people. Instead, what he got was a bullet in the gut from town marshal Frank Reid. Unfortunately, Frank wasn't fast enough; he died during his showdown with Soapy. Still, Soapy's presence made Skagway famous.

Today, there are only about 900 permanent residents in Skagway, and one of them is photographer Harry M. Walker.

"Skagway's main trade these days is tourism," he told me, over coffee in the Northern Lights Cafe, a restaurant on the town's main drag.

How did he get all the way to Alaska?

"I had originally come to Alaska to canoe the Yukon River," the bearded Walker continues. "I was working on a photo book about my experiences, and I liked the country so much I decided to stay."

Walker is a New Yorker. Before going to Alaska, he taught photography and also did public relations photography. He also points out proudly that he was a founding member of the Soho Photo Cooperative.

"I found a lot of opportunity for a New York trained photographer up here. I started out by continuing to do public relations photography in Anchorage, teaching, and I also began writing the first photography column in a local newspaper—in fact the first one in the state."

What Harry realized more and more was that he wanted to do what he describes as wilderness photography, everything from bears to flora, rock formations and rivers. But, he needed a way to support his photography "habit," short of staying a freelance photographer.

"I'd heard a lot about Skagway having tourist trade," he explains. Actually, what Harry had heard was cruise ships plying the waters off the Alaskan coast made regular stops during the summer months in Skagway.

"I figured it was the perfect locale for an old time picture studio, where people dress up in period costume and the photographer takes their picture. So, I established my business and it's given me a financial anchor, and I'm free part of the year to do the photography I really want to do."

Harry calculates that the studio remains open for 110 days. The rest of the time, he's free to take his wilderness photographs.

Perhaps there's nothing unique about Harry's experiences as a professional photographer. He left home for the dream of establishing a photography business he could live with; he wanted to shoot the type of pictures that gave him emotional fulfillment. Through perseverance, he achieved his goals. In the process, he also found a girl whom he loved and married.

The American dream? Maybe. But Harry was a professional photographer, already established, who decided to gamble even more.

It's like I said at the beginning of this book: if you want to make it, you have to take chances. Like Harry.

He made it. So can you. Keep looking for the green light.

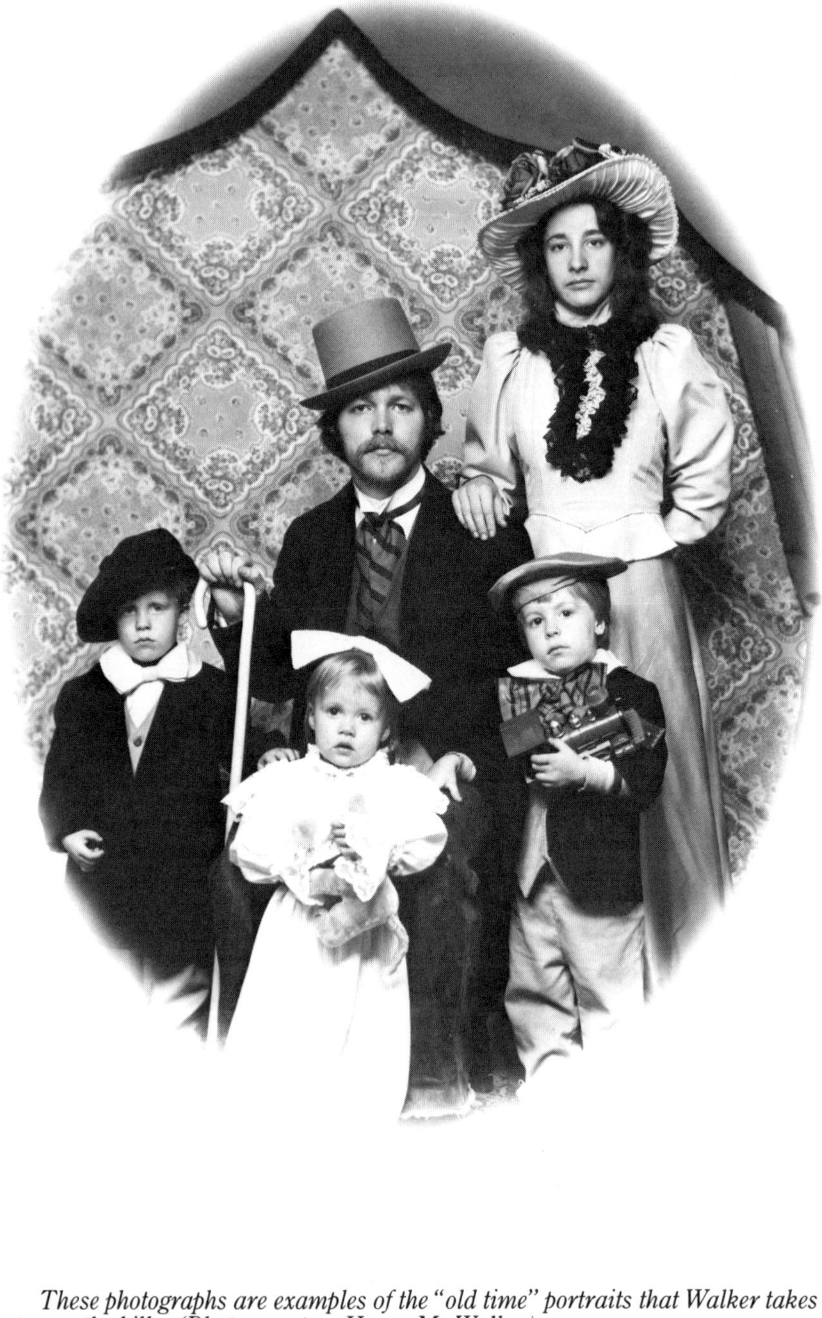

*These photographs are examples of the "old time" portraits that Walker takes to pay the bills. (Photo courtesy Harry M. Walker)*

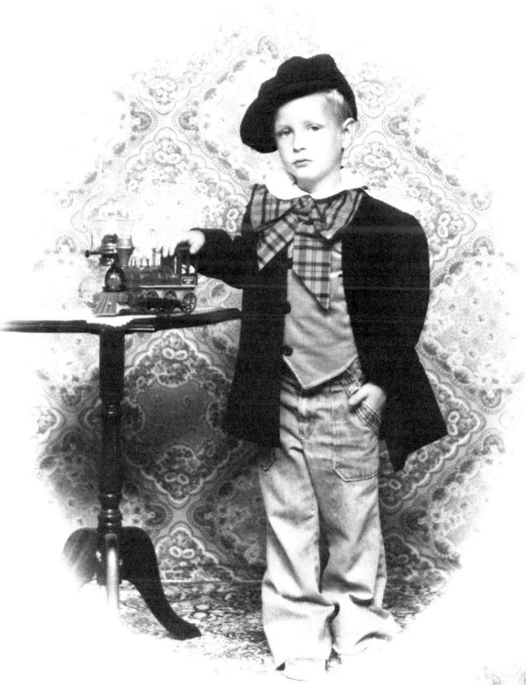

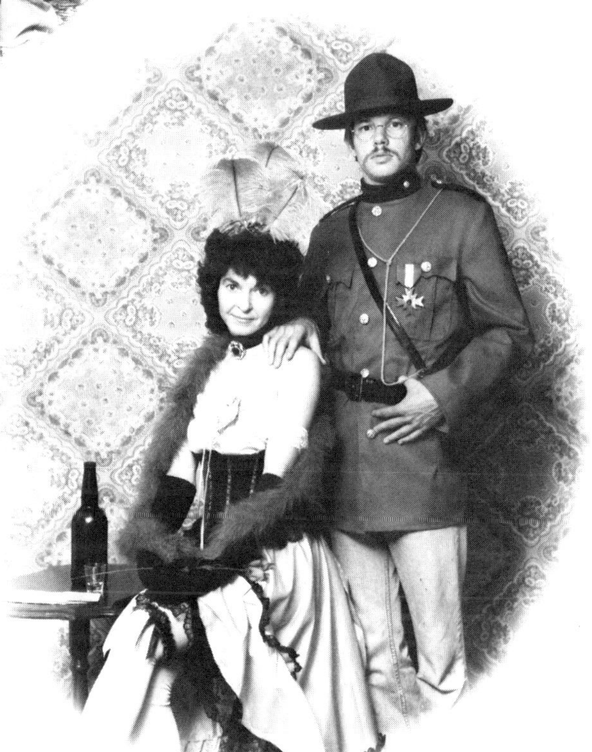

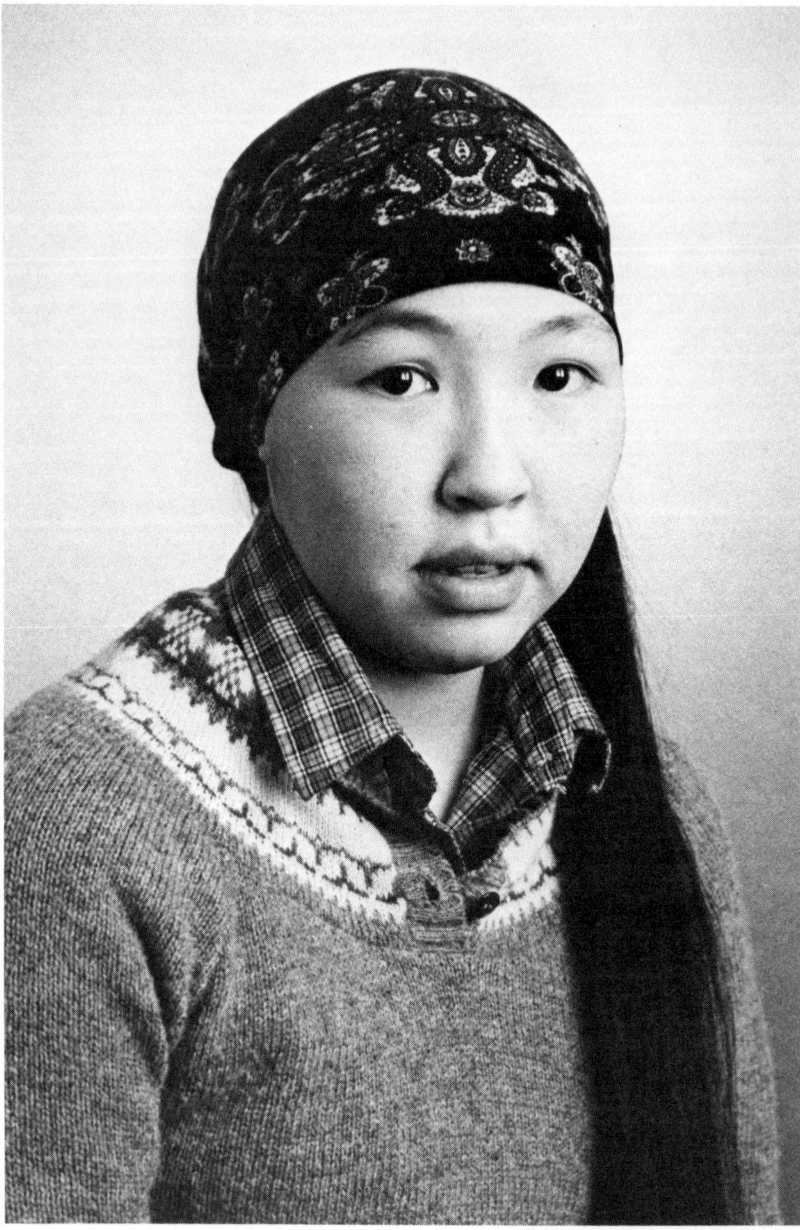

*These portraits of Yupik Eskimo were taken in Akiachak, Alaska. (Photo courtesy Harry M. Walker)*

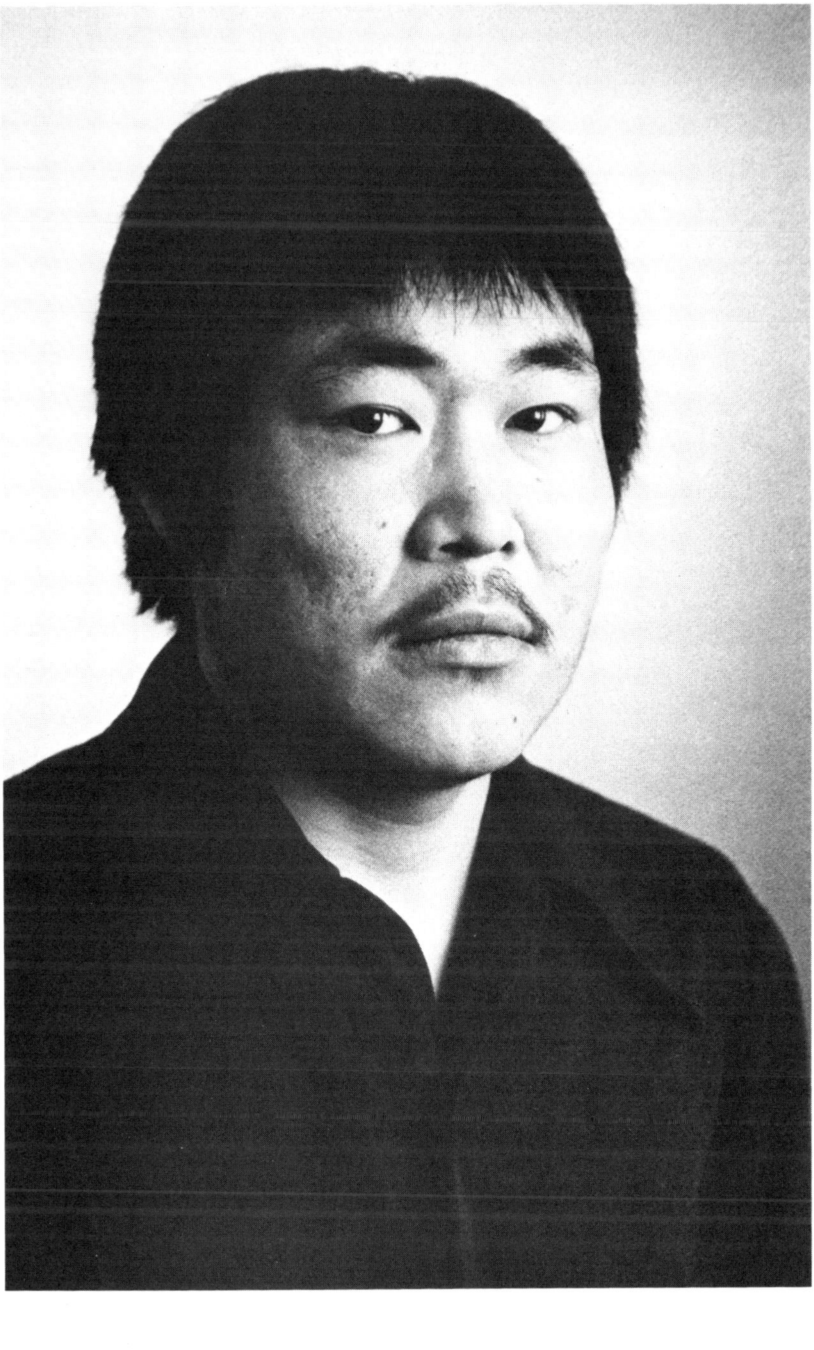

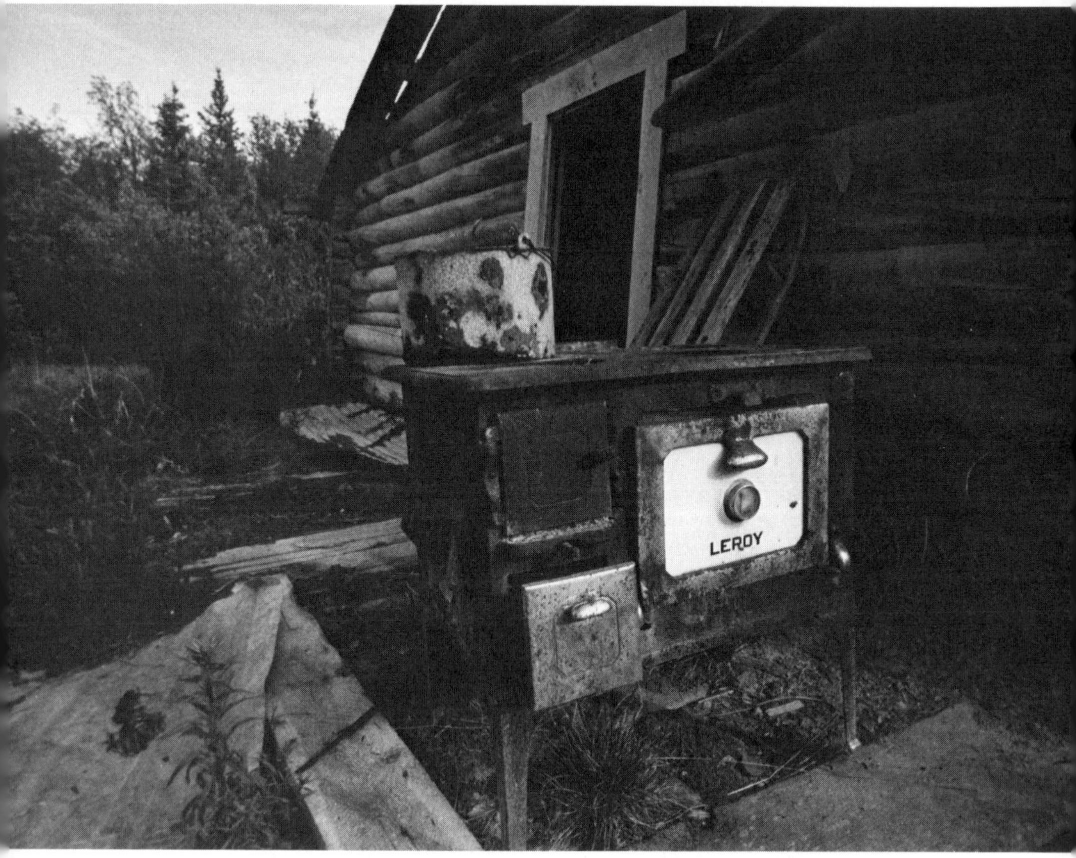


*Walker's first love—photographing nature, especially in the 49th state. (Photo courtesy Harry M. Walker)*

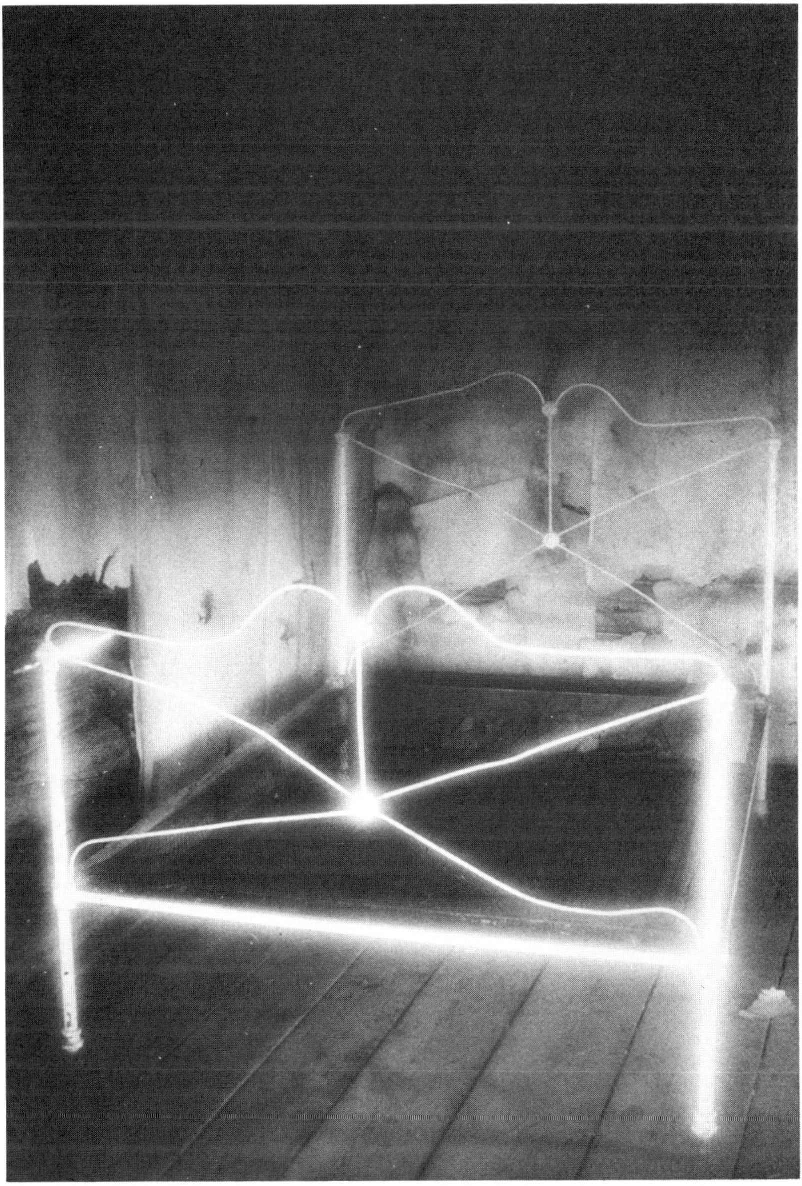

*This photograph illustrates Harry Walker's creative approach to photography. (Photo courtesy Harry M. Walker)*

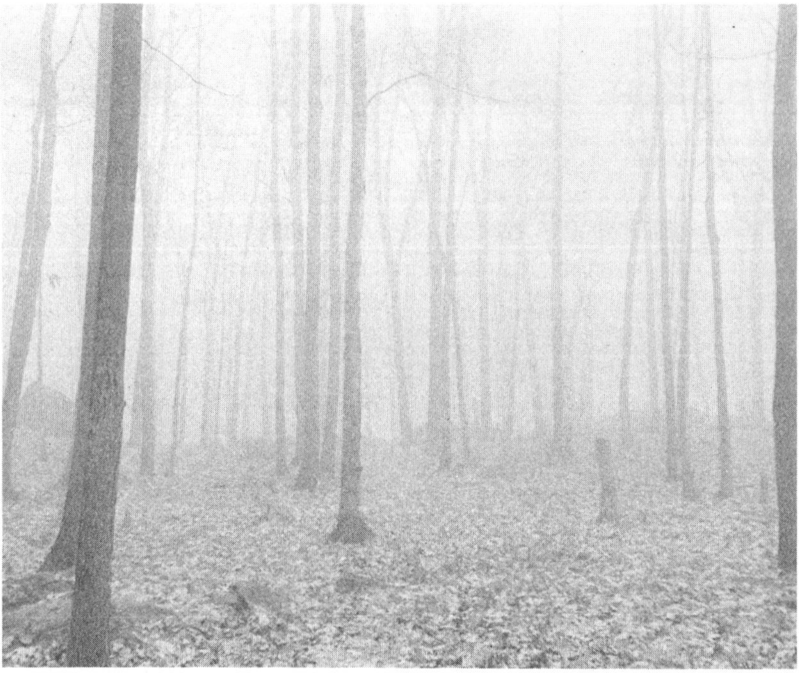

*Harriman State Park, New York (Photo courtesy Harry M. Walker)*

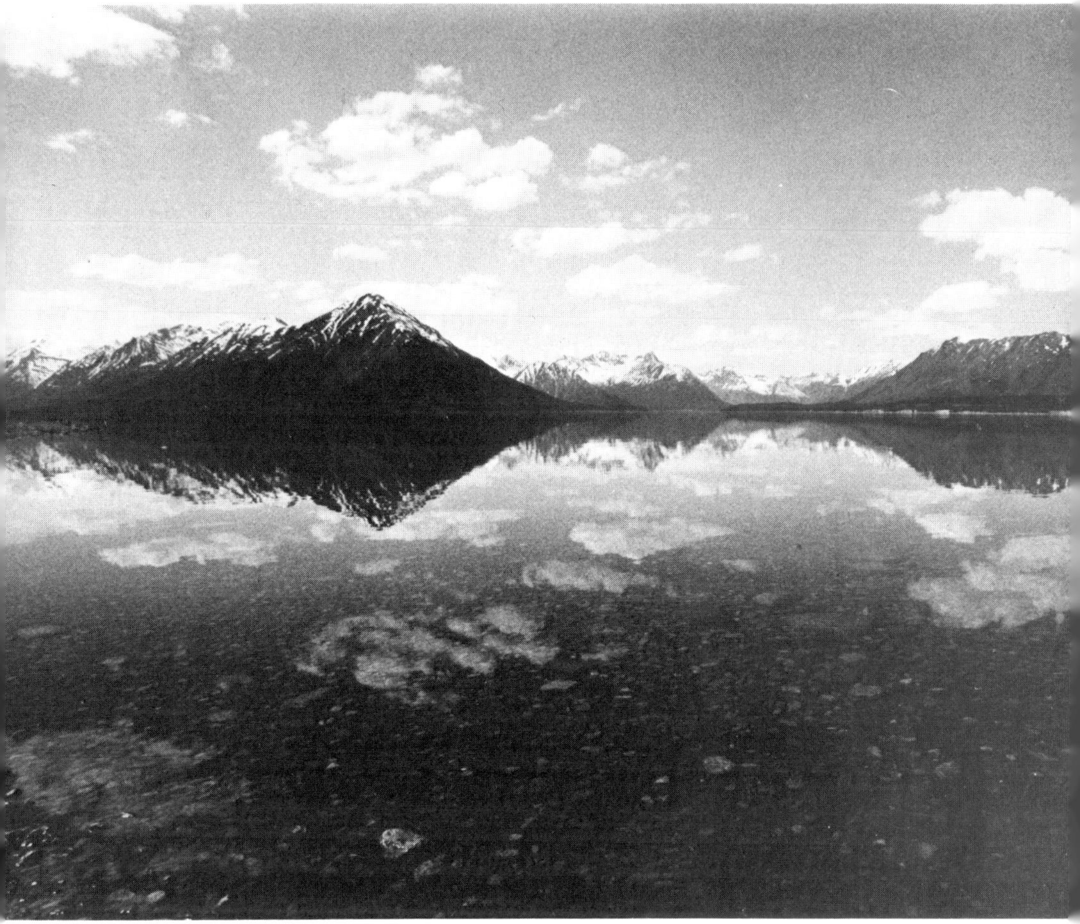

*Lake Bennett, British Columbia (Photo courtesy Harry M. Walker)*

# APPENDIXES

## APPENDIX A

# MARKETING RESOURCES AND PROMOTIONAL PUBLICATIONS

### PHOTOGRAPHER'S MARKET

Writer's Digest Books, 9933 Alliance Road, Cincinnati, Ohio 45242

*Photographer's Market* gives listings of magazines, newspapers, advertising agencies, public relations firms, and other sources of business that will buy your photographs. Details are given on the need and requirements of the company, the way to make contact, and in some instances, some helpful tips.

### WRITER'S MARKET

Writer's Digest Books (same address as above)

This publication lists (and gives an analysis of) markets for the writer, here in the United States, and in some cases, abroad. Each entry also lists the photographic requirements of the magazine. Contacting these publications by phone or mail will provide another marketing outlet for your photographs. This book also contains a detailed analysis of all the photography magazines mentioned in this book as well as some of the smaller ones I have left out.

## AMERICAN SHOWCASE

American Showcase Inc., 724 Fifth Avenue, New York, New York 10019

*American Showcase* is a full-color book that is used by advertising agencies and public relations firms who want to see examples of a photographer's work in print. Photographers who place their work in this publication do so that it will be seen by the people at these agencies who do the hiring. The photographer's name appears in the front of the book under an appropriate listing—but it costs. Essentially, a photographer's portfolio page in this publication is an advertisement, and the ad must be bought by the photographer. I think it's a good place for a photographer working in the commercial field to reach potential clients. Wedding and portrait photographers who want to stay in those fields might be wasting their money buying a page in this publication.

## THE CREATIVE BLACK BOOK

Creative Black Book, Inc., 401 Park Avenue South, New York, New York 10016

The *Creative Black Book* lists services an advertising agency needs—from photographers to make-up artists. Photographers may also purchase an ad in this publication, using a portfolio page that is similar to, or even the same as, the one used for *American Showcase.* Once again, it is an excellent place for a commercial photographer to advertise.

## PROFESSIONAL ORGANIZATIONS

Advertising Photographers of America
45 East 20th Street, New York, New York 10003

American Society of Magazine Photographers
205 Lexington Avenue, New York, New York 10016

Professional Photographers of America
1090 Executive Way, Des Plaines, Illinois 60018

# APPENDIX B
# MANUFACTURER INFORMATION

## CAMERA MANUFACTURERS

| | |
|---|---|
| Canon | Canon U.S.A., Inc.<br>One Canon Plaza, Lake Success, New York 11042 |
| Bronica | G.M.I. Photographic<br>P.O. Box Drawer U, Farmingdale, New York 11735 |
| Hasselblad | Victor Hasselblad, Inc.<br>10 Madison Road, Fairfield, New Jersey 07006 |
| Mamiya | Berkey Marketing Co.<br>25-20 Brooklyn-Queens Expressway, Woodside, New York 11377 |
| Minolta | Minolta Corporation<br>101 Williams Drive, Ramsey, New Jersey 07446 |
| Nikon | Nikon, Inc.<br>623 Stewart Avenue, Garden City, New York 11530 |

| | |
|---|---|
| Olympus | Olympus Corporation<br>Crossways Park, Woodbury, New York 11797 |
| Omega/View | Berkey Marketing Co.<br>25-20 Brooklyn-Queens Expressway, Woodside, New York 11377 |
| Pentax | Pentax Corporation<br>35 Iverness Dr. East, Englewood, Colorado 80112 |
| Rollei | Berkey Marketing Co.<br>(see Omega/View) |
| Sinar Bron | Sinar Bron<br>23 Progress Street, Edison, New Jersey 08820 |
| Soligor | AIC Photo Inc.<br>168 Glen Cove Road, Carle Place, New York 11514 |
| Vivitar | Vivitar Corporation<br>POB 2100, Santa Monica, California 90406 |

## FILM MANUFACTURERS

| | |
|---|---|
| Agfa | Agfa-Gevaert, Inc.<br>275 North Street, Teterboro, New Jersey 07608 |
| Fuji | Fuji Photo Film, U.S.A., Inc.<br>350 Fifth Avenue, New York, New York 10118 |
| Ilford | Ilford, Inc.<br>W. 70 Century Road, Paramus, New Jersey 07652 |
| Kodak | Eastman Kodak Co.<br>343 State Street, Rochester, New York 14650 |
| 3M | 3M Center<br>POB 33600, St. Paul, Minnesota 55133 |

## TRIPOD MANUFACTURERS

| | |
|---|---|
| Bogen | Bogen Photo Corporation<br>P.O. Box 712, Englewood, New Jersey 07140 |
| Gitzo | Karl Heitz<br>P.O. Box 427, Woodside, New York 11377 |

| | |
|---|---|
| Slik | Berkey Marketing Co.<br>25-20 Brooklyn-Queens Expressway, Woodside, New York 11377 |
| Tilt All | E. Leitz, Inc.<br>Link Dr., Rockleigh, New Jersey 07647 |

## LIGHTING MANUFACTURERS

| | |
|---|---|
| Balcar | Balcar Tekno<br>100 W. Erie Street, Chicago, Illinois 60610 |
| Speedotron | Speedotron Corporation<br>340 W. Huron Street, Chicago, Illinois 60610 |

## FILTER MANUFACTURERS

| | |
|---|---|
| Cokin | Minolta Corporation<br>101 Williams Drive, Ramsey, New Jersey 07446 |
| Tiffen | Tiffen<br>90 Oser Avenue, Hauppauge, New York 11788 |

## BACKGROUND PAPER MANUFACTURER

| | |
|---|---|
| Savage | Savage Universal Corporation<br>630 Third Avenue, New York, New York 10017 |

# INDEX

Edited by Marisa Bulzone and Donna Marcotrigiano
Designed by Jay Anning
Graphic Production by Hector Campbell
Jacket Photograph by Bill Smith